ROMAN POLANSKI

INTERVIEWS

CONVERSATIONS WITH FILMMAKERS SERIES
PETER BRUNETTE, GENERAL EDITOR

Photo credit: Photofest

ROMAN
POLANSKI
INTERVIEWS

EDITED BY PAUL CRONIN

UNIVERSITY PRESS OF MISSISSIPPI / JACKSON

www.upress.state.ms.us

The University Press of Mississippi is a member of the Association of American University Presses.

Manufactured in the United States of America

First edition 2005

∞

Library of Congress Cataloging-in-Publication Data

Roman Polanski : interviews / edited by Paul Cronin.— 1st ed.
       p. cm.
   Includes index.
   Filmography: p.
   ISBN 1-57806-799-5 (cloth : alk. paper) — ISBN 1-57806-800-2 (pbk. : alk. paper)
   1. Polanski, Roman—Interviews. 2. Motion picture producers and directors—United States—Interviews. I. Polanski, Roman. II. Cronin, Paul.
   PN1998.3.P65A3   2005
   791.4302′33′092—dc22   2005004457

British Library Cataloging-in-Publication Data available

C O N T E N T S

INTRODUCTION

WHEN SPEAKING RECENTLY to the French film magazine *Positif*, director Roman Polanski explained, "More than anything I just want to tell a good story. That's what drives me." And when it comes to this intricate craft, Polanski is a veritable polymath.

As an actor he was a fresh-faced nineteen-year-old in Andrzej Wajda's 1954 feature *A Generation*, and more than twenty years later appeared as the disturbed Trelkovsky in his own adaptation of *The Tenant*. He has contributed to or singlehandedly written the screenplays of every one of his ten short films and seventeen features, several of which he also produced. An eclectic body of work—in a 1984 interview presented here, Polanski explains that "I like cinema too much to be happy doing only one thing"—it includes a three-handed thriller filmed almost entirely on a small boat (*Knife in the Water*), a dark psychological study of descent into schizophrenia (*Repulsion*), a cartoon-inspired, genre-bending spoof vampire movie (*The Fearless Vampire Killers*), one of the most vibrant horror films mainstream Hollywood has ever produced (*Rosemary's Baby*), a bloodthirsty version of Shakespeare (*Macbeth*), a stylish *film noir* (*Chinatown*), a swashbuckling pirate story (*Pirates*), and an impassioned adaptation of Thomas Hardy (*Tess*). Polanski has also directed various operas and more recently appeared in several plays throughout Europe, while his autobiography (*Roman by Polanski*) is a fascinating and moving tale.

As the conversations in this book make clear, Polanski is a man very much enthralled by the opportunities the medium of film offers the storyteller. He reveals to more than one interviewer that it isn't literature or fine art that serve as his points of references—it is cinema, most importantly those films that have resonated strongly with him. Reed's *Odd Man Out*, Olivier's *Hamlet*, Kurosawa's *Rashomon*, Laughton's *Night of the Hunter*, and Fellini's *8½*—all are cited repeatedly. Polanski can even pinpoint the moment he realized film was something special for him, recalling to *Le Nouvel Observateur* in 1984 that when living in the Krakow ghetto—the liquidation of which he was lucky to survive— the Germans "sometimes showed films outside in the market-place, on the other side from where we lived, and I would watch the projection through barbed wire. It was generally Third Reich propaganda with the intermission consisting of slides which had things like 'Jews = Typhoid' on them. When the Soviets arrived they inundated us with their patriotic films and I was immediately converted."

Fortunately for Polanski and his contemporaries, postwar Poland boasted one of the finest film schools in the world, and in interviews over the past forty years Polanski has frequently spoken of the training—and the freedom—he was given at the film school in Lodz where he spent five years. "Lenin said cinema was the most important art form that existed, something that gave a lot of prestige to filmmakers," he informed *Cahiers du Cinéma* in 1992. "This meant the Communists didn't dare interfere too much with us." When interviewed by *L'avant-scène cinema* in 1983, Polanski confesses, "We never stopped complaining about how much time we were wasting—and those five years did seem like a very long time. But I quickly realized how much I actually owe to the school. There's no doubt it's where I learned my job."

Polanski's time at Lodz, with its immersion in the practical side of filmmaking, is perhaps one reason why he is so reticent to "explain" his films. The filmmaker we meet in this book is a man unlikely ever to assist interviewers in identifying the themes that might be found running through his body of work. In 1966, *Les lettres françaises* learned that for Polanski, "a film is like a painting or a sculpture—it's something to be looked at, not talked about," and in 1999 the German newspaper *Die Woche* quoted the director as saying that it wasn't "this whole 'art' cinema thing and the philosophical depth of filmmaking that interest me. That doesn't matter to me at all. I simply like to play with the camera, the lights, the actors. To me, filmmaking is what a train set is to a child." Polanski's intensive technical training and wide knowledge of the filmmaking process might also explain his dismissive attitude of a figure like John Cassavetes, an actor with whom he worked on *Rosemary's Baby*. By 1968 Cassavetes had directed two highly regarded "independent" productions, elements of which were rooted in earlier unstructured improvisations. But as *Positif* discovered in 1969, to Polanski's mind Cassavetes is "not a filmmaker—he's made some films, that's all. Anyone could take a camera and do what he did with *Shadows*."

However valuable his film school training, however much Lodz proved to be an island of freedom in the sea of Stalinism that was communist Poland, Polanski was from the start determined to escape the Iron Curtain. Reluctant to discuss politics with any of the interviewers in this book (*Le Nouvel Observateur*, 1984: "I've tried to stay clear of politics as much as possible ever since I became disillusioned twenty-five years ago when living in Poland"), Polanski's attitude to his homeland is nevertheless revealing. "Poland was a cramped and unpleasant country, and cinema had no future there," he tells *Cahiers du Cinéma*. In 1984, Polanski disclosed that his drive for success led him to act out "for real what my compatriots only dreamt about. Most of them were happy to live in the West only in their minds, but I was raring to escape as soon as I could, no matter what. I even imagined building a pedal-powered submarine." One of cinema's most itinerant directors, Polanski tells Franz-Olivier Giesbert, "I've always considered myself a nomad," and with an adventurous spirit in 1979 explained to *Cahiers du Cinéma*, "I don't know why I should especially associate myself with any particular country just because of where I was born or educated."

After spending some years in England where he made *Repulsion* and *Cul-de-sac* ("the happiest times of my life"), Polanski reached Hollywood in the late 1960s. Although many of the films he cites as strong influences on his own films are American (particularly Welles's *Citizen Kane*, "a blueprint of how cinema should be"), Polanski has had something of an ambivalent relationship with Hollywood (an "intellectual desert") and the United States in general. Throughout his conversations with journalists since leaving that country for good in the late 1970s, Polanski has spoken of his deep affection for Europe, especially Paris (a "heaven on earth"). His first contact with Hollywood came during the production (in England) of *The Fearless Vampire Killers* in 1967 for MGM. He was denied final cut in America, and the version released there was the producer's, a man who insisted he was more savvy than Polanski when it came to marketing. But he was, as the director lamented to Michael Delahaye and Jean Narboni in 1969, "absolutely intent on spoiling the film."

A year later Polanski was transfixed by the unpublished manuscript of Ira Levin's novel *Rosemary's Baby*. "I went straight to the studio and told them I was really interested in doing it, but on one condition: the story stays as it is and they don't try to improve it. That's what they always do in Hollywood—try to improve great scripts that then turn out terribly" (Delahaye and Narboni). Looking back fifteen years later, Polanski felt that "Hollywood is a land of leisure that you can blend into within 24 hours. But quite quickly I realized that the studios are run by a bunch of agents and lawyers who don't have much to do with the artistic side of things. The gulf between these people and the artists is constantly widening and their relationships can be so fraught that you wonder if some filmmakers haven't purposely tried to bankrupt their producers" (Giesbert).

Polanski's dislike of the bureaucracy filmmaking entails and his interests in areas other than cinema (the director on Stanley Kubrick, as recorded by *The Dick Cavett Show*: "he's very interested in every-thing—like I am, by the way") meant that despite the critical and commercial success of *Tess* in 1980, Polanski expressed a strong desire to quit filmmaking. "The film industry has fallen into the hands of profiteers who are only interested in prestige, honor and, to put it crudely, cheap sex. I would only get involved with those people again if I found a film project that was very close to my heart," Polanski told *Le Matin de Paris*, adding several years later that "Making films is a battle, and sometimes one tires of fighting" (*Die Woche*). Yet only a few years later, Polanski was to be found in Tunisia hard at work on *Pirates*, his long-cherished project that was finally released in 1986. More recently, Polanski has achieved success in Hollywood with his wartime drama *The Pianist*, a film that won a succession of important awards around the world and that he discusses here in conversation with Spanish writer and Holocaust survivor Jorge Semprun.

In keeping with other books in the University Press of Mississippi series, all interviews in this book are presented in chronological order. Though there have been many published interviews with Polanski in several languages stretching back at least as far as 1960, I have generally avoided using profiles and articles that include quotes from the director, preferring instead to use pieces in the Q&A format. As Polanski said in a recent feature about him published in England, "The ways of your journalists are mysterious. In France they treat me with respect, they ask me about my films." This is why this volume contains new translations of interviews originally published in Spanish, German, and, importantly, French, all of which have been edited to make them as coherent as possible when presented here. It is also why this book is about Polanski the filmmaker, and not (to quote from the man's autobiography) Polanski the "evil, profligate dwarf."

Thanks to Peter Brunette, to Seetha Srinivasan, Anne Stascavage, and Walter Biggins at the University Press of Mississippi, and to Roman Polanski and Isobelle Dassonville. Thanks also to Jerica Kraljic, Tamara Kraljic, Moritz Gimbel, Marie-Antoinette Guillochon, Angelina Guillochon-Perez, Joshua Kronen, Marcos Pérez-Navarrete, and especially Remi Guillochon who all gave invaluable translating assistance. This book is for Leo Cronin, first of the new generation, and Jeremy Freeson, a trusted friend.

CHRONOLOGY

1933	Born in Paris on 18 August to Ryszard, a Polish Jew, and Bula (*née* Katz), a Russian Jew.
1936	Family moves to Krakow, Poland.
1942	Bula Polanski dies at Auschwitz.
1943	Escapes the Krakow ghetto and hides in the Polish country-side with a series of Catholic families.
1945	Reunited with his father.
1947	Wins prize for his appearance in the stage production *Son of the Regiment*.
1949	Appears in *Circus Tarabumba* at the Krakow Puppet Theatre.
1950	Transfers from technical college to art school.
1953	Graduates art school. Rejected from Krakow Drama School. First film appearance as an actor, in *Three Stories*, a compilation film produced at the Polish Film School in Lodz.
1954	Appears in Andrzej Wajda's *A Generation*. Begins studies at Polish Film School.
1955	Unfinished short *Bicycle*.
1958	Short *Two Men and a Wardrobe* receives Honorable Mention at the Oberhausen Short Film Festival, the Bronze Medal at the Brussels Film Festival and the Golden Gate award at the San Francisco International Festival.
1959	Graduation film *When Angels Fall*. Assists director Andrzej Munk on *Bad Luck*. Marries Barbara Kwiatkowska and spends a year in Paris where he meets future writing partner Gérard Brach. Appears in Andrzej Wajda's *Lotna*.
1961	Divorces Barbara Kwiatkowska. Makes *The Fat and the Lean* in Paris.

1962   Feature debut *Knife in the Water* nominated for Best Foreign Film Academy Award.

1963   One of four directors to contribute a segment to *The Beautiful Swindlers*.

1964   *Do You Like Women?*, directed by Jean Léon, from a script by Polanski and Brach, adapted from the novel by Georges Bardawil.

1965   In London shoots *Repulsion*, which wins Silver Bear at Berlin Film Festival.

1966   *Cul-de-sac*, filmed in England, wins Golden Bear at Berlin Film Festival.

1967   Directs and stars, alongside Sharon Tate, in *The Fearless Vampire Killers* for MGM. Jean-Michel Simon directs *The Girl Across the Way* from a script by Polanski and Brach.

1968   Shoots *Rosemary's Baby* for Paramount. The film is condemned by the Catholic Legion of Decency and cut by British censors. Marries Sharon Tate in London. Clashes with French directors Truffaut and Godard at the Cannes Film Festival.

1969   Sharon Tate, pregnant at the time, murdered in Los Angeles.

1970   Moves to Rome. *A Day at the Beach* directed by Simon Hesera, from a Polanski script.

1971   Films *Macbeth* in England from a script co-written with critic Kenneth Tynan. *Boat on the Grass*, directed by Gérard Brach, from a Polanski/Brach script.

1972   Produces and appears in documentary *Weekend of a Champion*, about racing driver Jackie Stewart.

1973   Directs *What?* in Italy for producer Carlo Ponti.

1974   Directs *Chinatown* for Paramount. Directs Alban Berg's opera *Lulu* in Italy.

1975   Directs Verdi's opera *Rigoletto* in Germany.

1976   Adapts (from Roland Topor's novel), directs, and appears in *The Tenant*, filmed in Paris.

1977   Arrested in Los Angeles on charges of unlawful sexual intercourse with thirteen-year old girl. Given a ninety-day jail sentence for diagnostic purposes.

1978   Leaves the United States for Paris, via London.

1979	*Tess*, filmed in France, wins César Awards for Best Film and Best Director.
1981	Directs and appears in Peter Schaffer's play *Amadeus* in Warsaw.
1982	Brings *Amadeus* to Paris.
1984	Publishes autobiography, *Roman by Polanski.*
1986	*Pirates*, starring Walter Matthau, filmed in Tunisia.
1987	Directs and appears in Peter Schaffer's play *The Royal Hunt of the Sun* in Paris.
1988	Shoots *Frantic* in Paris starring Harrison Ford and Emmanuelle Seigner. Appears in Steven Berkoff's stage adaptation of Kafka's *Metamorphosis* in Paris.
1989	Marries Emmanuelle Seigner.
1992	Films *Bitter Moon* with Emmanuelle Seigner in Paris. Stages Offenbach's opera *The Tales of Hoffman* in Paris.
1994	Adapts Ariel Dorfman's play *Death and the Maiden* starring Ben Kingsley.
1996	Film project *The Double*, to have starred John Travolta, is abandoned. Short film *Gli Angeli*.
1997	Musical version of *The Fearless Vampire Killers* opens in Vienna.
1999	Releases *The Ninth Gate*, filmed in Paris, starring Johnny Depp.
2002	*The Pianist*, based on the book by Wladyslaw Szpilman and with a script by Ronald Harwood, wins Palme d'Or at Cannes Film Festival and Academy Award for Best Director.
2003	Directs Ibsen's *Hedda Gabler* in Paris, starring Emmanuelle Seigner.
2005	*Oliver Twist*, featuring Ben Kingsley and adapted by Ronald Harwood from the Charles Dickens novel, is released.

FILMOGRAPHY

1955
BICYCLE (ROWER) [unfinished]
Producer: Panstwowa Wyzsza Szkola Filmowa (Polish Film School)
Director: **Polanski**
Screenplay: **Polanski**
Cinematography: Nikola Todorov
Cast: Adam Fiut, **Polanski**

1957
TEETH SMILE (USMIECH ZEBICZNY)
Producer: Panstwowa Wyzsza Szkola Filmowa (Polish Film School)
Director: **Polanski**
Screenplay: **Polanski**
Cinematography: Henryk Kucharski
Cast: Nikola Todorov
2 minutes

BREAKING UP THE DANCE (ROZBIJEMY ZABAWE)
Producer: Panstwowa Wyzsza Szkola Filmowa (Polish Film School)
Director: **Polanski**
Screenplay: **Polanski**
Cinematography: Marek Nowicki, Andrzej Galinski
8 minutes

MURDERER (MORDERSTWO)
Producer: Panstwowa Wyzsza Szkola Filmowa (Polish Film School)
Director: **Polanski**

Screenplay: **Polanski**
Cinematography: Nikola Todorov
2 minutes (silent)

1958
TWO MEN AND A WARDROBE (DWAJ LUDZIE Z SZAFA)
Producer: Panstwowa Wyzsza Szkola Filmowa (Polish Film School)
Director: **Polanski**
Screenplay: **Polanski**
Cinematography: Maciej Kijowski
Cast: Jakuba Goldberg, Henryka Klube, Andrzej Kondratiuk, Barbara Kwiatkowska, Stanislaw Michalski, **Polanski**
15 minutes

1959
LAMPA (THE LAMP)
Producer: Panstwowa Wyzsza Szkola Filmowa (Polish Film School)
Director: **Polanski**
Screenplay: **Polanski**
Cinematography: Krzysztof Romanowski
7 minutes

WHEN ANGELS FALL (GDY SPADAJA ANJOLY)
Producer: Panstwowa Wyzsza Szkola Filmowa (Polish Film School)
Director: **Polanski**
Screenplay: **Polanski**
Cinematography: Henryk Kucharski
Cast: Barbara Kwiatkowska, Andrzej Kondratiuk, Henryka Klube, **Polanski**, Andrzej Kostenko
21 minutes

1961
THE FAT AND THE LEAN (GRUBY I CHUDY)
Producer: Claude Joudioux (A. P. E. C)
Director: **Polanski**

Screenplay: **Polanski**
Cinematography: Jean-Michel Trzcinski
Cast: Andrzej Katelbach, **Polanski**
15 minutes

1962
MAMMALS (SSAKI)
Producer: Wotjek Frykowski (Films Polski)
Director: **Polanski**
Screenplay: Andrzej Kondratiuk, **Polanski**
Cinematography: Andrzej Kostenko
Cast: Henryka Klube, Michal Zolnierkiewicz
10 minutes

KNIFE IN THE WATER (NÓZ W WODZIE)
Producer: Stanislaw Zylewicz (Films Polski)
Director: **Polanski**
Screenplay: Jakuba Goldberg, **Polanski**, Jerzy Skolimowski
Cinematography: Jerzy Lipman
Editor: Halina Prugar-Ketting
Cast: Zygmunt Malanowicz (Young Boy), Leon Neimczyk (Andrzej),
Jolanta Umecka (Krystyna)
94 minutes

1964
THE RIVER OF DIAMONDS [segment of THE BEAUTIFUL SWINDLERS]
Producer: Pierre Roustang (Ulysse Productions, Primex Films)
Director: **Polanski**
Screenplay: **Polanski**, Gérard Brach
Cinematography: Jerzy Lipman
Editor: Rita van Royen
Cast: Nicole Karen, Jan Teulings, Arnold Gelderman
33 minutes

1965
REPULSION
Producers: Tony Tenser, Michael Klinger, Gene Gutowski (Compton
Films, Tekli Films)

Director: **Polanski**
Screenplay: Gérard Brach, **Polanski**, David Stone (adaptation)
Cinematography: Gilbert Taylor
Editor: Alastair McIntyre
Cast: Catherine Deneuve (Carole), Ian Hendry (Michael), John Fraser (Colin), Yvonne Furneaux (Helen), Patrick Wymark (Landlord)
104 minutes

1966
CUL-DE-SAC
Producers: Tony Tenser, Michael Klinger, Gene Gutowski (Compton Films, Teki Films)
Director: **Polanski**
Screenplay: Gérard Brach, **Polanski**
Cinematography: Gilbert Taylor
Editor: Alastair McIntyre
Cast: Donald Pleasence (George), Françoise Dorléac (Teresa), Lionel Stander (Richard), Jack MacGowran (Albie), Iain Quarrier (Christopher), Geoffrey Sumner (Christopher's father), Renee Houston (Christopher's mother)
111 minutes

1967
THE FEARLESS VAMPIRE KILLERS
Producer: Gene Gutowski (Metro-Goldwyn-Mayer)
Director: **Polanski**
Screenplay: Gérard Brach, **Polanski**
Cinematography: Douglas Slocombe
Editor: Alastair McIntyre
Cast: Jack MacGowran (Professor Abronsius), **Polanski** (Alfred), Alfie Bass (Shagal), Jessie Robins (Rebecca Shagal), Sharon Tate (Sarah Shagal), Ferdy Mayne (Count Von Krolock), Iain Quarrier (Herbert Von Krolock), Terry Downes (Koukol)
124 minutes

1968
ROSEMARY'S BABY
Producer: William Castle (Paramount Pictures)
Director: **Polanski**

Screenplay: **Polanski** (based on the novel by Ira Levin)
Cinematography: William Fraker
Editors: Sam O'Steen, Bob Wyman
Cast: Mia Farrow (Rosemary Woodhouse), John Cassavetes (Guy Woodhouse), Ruth Gordon (Minnie Castevet), Sidney Blackmer (Roman Castevet), Maurice Evans (Hutch), Ralph Bellamy (Dr. Sapirstein), Victoria Vetri (Terry), Patsy Kelly (Laura-Louise), Elisha Cook Jr. (Mr. Nicklas), Emmaline Henry (Elise Dunstan), Charles Grodin (Dr. Hill)
136 minutes

1971
MACBETH
Producer: Andrew Braunsberg (Playboy Production, Caliban Films)
Director: **Polanski**
Screenplay: **Polanski**, Kenneth Tynan (based on the play by William Shakespeare)
Cinematography: Gilbert Taylor
Editor: Alastair McIntyre
Cast: Jon Finch (Macbeth), Francesca Annis (Lady Mabeth), Martin Shaw (Banquo), Nicholas Selby (Duncan), John Stride (Ross), Stephen Chase (Malcolm), Paul Shelley (Donalbain), Terence Bayer (Macduff)
140 minutes

1973
WHAT?
Producer: Carlo Ponti (C. C. Champion, Les Films Concordia, Dieter Geissler)
Director: **Polanski**
Screenplay: Gérard Brach, **Polanski**
Cinematography: Marcello Gatti, Giuseppe Ruzzolini
Editor: Alastair McIntyre
Cast: Marcello Mastroianni (Alex), Sydne Rome (Nancy), Hugh Griffith (Noblart), Henning Schlüter (Catone)
112 minutes

1974
CHINATOWN
Producer: Robert Evans (Paramount Pictures)

Director: **Polanski**
Screenplay: Robert Towne
Cinematography: John Alonzo
Editor: Sam O'Steen
Cast: Jack Nicholson (Jake Gittes), Faye Dunaway (Evelyn Cross Mulwray), John Huston (Noah Cross), Perry Lopez (Lieutenant Lou Escobar), John Hillerman (Russ Yelburton), Darrell Zwerling (Hollis Mulwray), Diane Ladd (Ida Sessions), Roy Jenson (Claude Mulvihill), **Polanski** (Man with Knife), Richard Bakalyan (Detective Loach), Joe Mantell (Lawrence Walsh), Bruce Glover (Duffy), James Hong (Kahn)
130 minutes

1976
THE TENANT
Producer: Andrew Braunsberg (Marianne Productions)
Director: **Polanski**
Screenplay: Gérard Brach, **Polanski** (based on the novel by Roland Topor)
Cinematography: Sven Nykvist
Editor: Françoise Bonnot
Cast: **Polanski** (Trelkovsky), Isabelle Adjani (Stella), Melvyn Douglas (Monsieur Zy), Jo Van Fleet (Madame Dioz), Bernard Fresson (Scope), Lila Kedrova (Madame Gaderian)
126 minutes

1979
TESS
Producers: Claude Berri, Timothy Burill (Remm Productions, Burill Productions)
Director: **Polanski**
Screenplay: Gérard Brach, John Brownjohn, **Polanski** (based on the novel by Thomas Hardy)
Cinematography: Ghislain Cloquet, Geoffrey Unsworth
Editors: Alastair McIntyre, Tom Priestly
Cast: Nastassia Kinski (Tess), Peter Firth (Angel Clare), Leigh Lawson (Alex d'Uberville), John Collin (Jack Durbeyfield), Tony Church (Tringham), Arielle Dombasle (Mercy Chant)
165 minutes

1986
PIRATES
Producer: Tarak Ben Ammar (Carthago Films)
Director: **Polanski**
Screenplay: Gérard Brach, John Brownjohn, **Polanski**
Cinematography: Witold Sobocinski
Editors: Hervé de Luze, William Reynolds
Cast: Walter Matthau (Captain Thomas Bartholomew Red), Cris
Campion (The Frog), Damien Thomas (Don Alfonso)
124 minutes

1988
FRANTIC
Producers: Tim Hampton, Thom Mount (Warner Bros.)
Director: **Polanski**
Screenplay: Gérard Brach, **Polanski**
Cinematography: Witold Sobocinski
Editor: Sam O'Steen
Cast: Harrison Ford (Richard Walker), Emmanuelle Seigner (Michelle),
Betty Buckley (Sondra Walker)
120 minutes

1992
BITTER MOON
Producers: **Polanski**, Alain Sarde (R. P. Productions, Burrill Productions)
Director: **Polanski**
Screenplay: Gérard Brach, John Brownjohn, **Polanski** (based on the
novel by Pascal Bruckner)
Cinematography: Tonino Delli Colli
Editor: Hervé de Luze
Cast: Hugh Grant (Nigel), Kristin Scott Thomas (Fiona), Emmanuelle
Seigner (Mimi), Peter Coyote (Oscar), Victor Banerjee (Mr. Singh),
Sophie Patel (Amrita), Stockard Channing (Beverly)
138 minutes

1994
DEATH AND THE MAIDEN
Producers: Thom Mount, Josh Kramer (Capitol Films, Mount/Kramer)

Director: **Polanski**
Screenplay: Rafael Yglesias, Ariel Dorfman (based on the play by Ariel
Dorfman)
Cinematography: Tonino Delli Colli
Editor: Hervé de Luze
Cast: Sigourney Weaver (Paulina Escobar), Ben Kingsley (Roberto
Miranda), Stuart Wilson (Gerardo Escobar)
103 minutes

1999
THE NINTH GATE
Producer: **Polanski** (Artisan Entertainment)
Director: **Polanski**
Screenplay: John Brownjohn, Enrique Urbizu, **Polanski** (based on the
novel by Arturo Pérez-Reverte)
Cinematography: Darius Khondj
Editor: Hervé de Luze
Cast: Johnny Depp (Dean Corso), Frank Langella (Boris Balkan), Lena
Olin (Liana Telfer), Emmanuelle Seigner (The Girl), Barbara Jefford
(Baroness Kessler), Jack Taylor (Victor Fargas)
133 minutes

2002
THE PIANIST
Producers: Robert Benmussa, **Polanski**, Alain Sarde (Canal+, Studio
Babelsberg)
Director: **Polanski**
Screenplay: Ronald Harwood (based on the novel by Wladyslaw
Szpilman)
Cinematography: Pawel Edelman
Editor: Hervé de Luze
Cast: Adrien Brody (Wladyslaw Szpilman), Thomas Kretschmann
(Captain Wilm Hosenfeld), Emilia Fox (Dorota), Ed Stoppard
(Henryk), Maureen Lipman (Mother), Frank Finlay (Father), Julia
Raynor (Regina)
148 minutes

2005
OLIVER TWIST
Producers: Robert Benmussa, Timothy Burrill, **Polanski**, Alain Sarde
Director: **Polanski**
Screenplay: Ronald Harwood (based on the novel by Charles Dickens)
Cinematography: Pawel Edelman
Editor: Hervé de Luze
Cast: Ben Kingsley (Fagin), Barney Clarke (Oliver Twist), Edward
Hardwicke (Mr. Brownlow), Jamie Foreman (Bill Sykes), Harry Eden
(The Artful Dodger), Leanne Rowe (Nancy), Lewis Chase (Charley
Bates), Jeremy Swift (Mr. Bumble), Mark Strong (Toby Crackit), Frances
Cuka (Mrs. Bedwin), Chris Overton (Noah Claypole), Michael Heath
(Mr. Sowerberry), Gillian Hanna (Mrs. Sowerberry)

ROMAN POLANSKI

INTERVIEWS

Roman Polanski

SCRIPT/1963

BACK IN THE DAYS when I was at film school—I think it's different today—we made two silent films of two or three minutes each during the first year. In the third year we made a documentary, and in the fourth a fiction film. Throughout year five we made our diploma project, the length of which was between 300 and 600 metres. Aside from those requirements, we also worked on other films, for example my own short *Two Men and a Wardrobe*.

Before I made *Two Men and a Wardrobe* I'd already made *The Bike*, but it was never finished because the lab accidentally sent a reel of the negative to Moscow where the Youth Festival was taking place, and it was never seen again. The film was in color, and I think it would have been quite good. I did make another film in color, *When Angels Fall*, which was my diploma film.

Although it was never my intention, *Two Men and a Wardrobe* is rather symbolic. Two men come out of the sea carrying a wardrobe and walk into town. People can't stand the sight of them traipsing around with this thing, especially when they go into cafés or try to get onto a tram. They stick out and because of this provoke hatred wherever they go. I wanted to show the unpleasant things going on in town around the two of them, all these crimes that no one does anything about because everyone's focused on these two strangers. No one says anything to the murderer or the boys who kill the cat, but at the same

From *Script*, May 1963. Reprinted by permission of Jo Gryn, publishing editor. Translated by Paul Cronin and Remi Guillochon.

time they can't tolerate this bizarre trio of two men and the wardrobe who end up just walking back into the ocean.

Of course, that's my version. Every audience member will presumably come up with something completely different. But it's a film, not an article in a political journal or newspaper imbued with an ideology or philosophy.

The Fat and the Lean is the story of a man enslaved. The idea is simply that of someone being tormented and made to endure harsher and harsher suffering, and who is eventually happy to return to his original hardships. It's similar to the story of the man who bangs his head against a wall. When asked why, he explains, "Because it feels so good when I stop."

I don't have any preferences for shooting on location—it depends on the story. I'm inspired by what I find on film sets. With *The Fat and the Lean*, for example, it was important that the man escaped into a flat landscape because then we can see that the place he's running to—the town, this oasis—is so far away. The story couldn't take place in a house where all he would have to do is open and close a door.

I need a situation or characters in order to write a screenplay. The most important thing, whether it's cinema or theater, where someone is playing a part (abstract films don't count), is character. The character, even if it's a dog, is always at the center of the story. Dramatic situations are quickly forgotten but characters stay with us. A good film is always about its characters, whether we're watching Charles Chaplin, James Dean, or James Stewart. For a novel, the writer finds an interesting character he wants to describe and only then creates the story around this person.

Apparently some authors—and this applies to painters too—don't know what they're going to do before they start. They just do it. The results can be astounding, but that's not my way of working. For my short films I always outlined the editing very accurately by making storyboards of each shot, though this never stopped me from changing things at the last minute. Why not make use of whatever arises on location? I didn't plan each shot with as much care for *Knife in the Water* because it would have been too time-consuming and I couldn't be bothered. Also because it's just not possible to have control over absolutely everything. The story takes place on a tiny yacht and the situations between the characters are limited. I had to approach it much more in terms of improvisation, and it helped to make only basic sketches of the shots.

Not using direct sound in my short films was never a financial consideration. There are some films where music works better than everyday noises. To include every single sound means a film becomes realistic and concrete, leaving nothing to the imagination. It's not a good idea to include both music and sound effects—you have to choose between them. My short films are not at all realistic so I wanted music in them. I asked a musician whom I've known for a long time to compose something that would express the feelings behind the images. If I'd got rid of the music, I would have added only sound effects and the audience would have wondered why the characters never spoke out loud. But if I'd written dialogue, the story would have become uninteresting. When something is expressed too clearly, it can fall flat.

Cinema isn't like chemistry where you can predict that ten grams of one substance, when combined with five grams of another, will give a particular result. With cinema, I do as I please. When I started at film school everyone had their own theories, but today this is precisely what I mistrust more than anything else. You can't make films with theories, except for things like *Last Year in Marienbad* which is far too serious for me.

Everything in this life has a comic quality on the surface and a tragic quality underneath. Comic episodes often hide supposedly serious incidents. It's the kind of thing that happens at a funeral or even in a concentration camp. I think that in spite of their great suffering, the prisoners laughed from time to time because of these moments of comedy. There's a lot of literature in this vein. Personally, I can't stand overly serious films like [Kaneto Shindo's 1961 film] *The Naked Island*. Besides, they aren't very good films. Life like this just doesn't exist, just as you'd never encounter the kinds of situations you see in *Last Year in Marienbad.*

I worked as an actor—not an assistant—for Andrzej Wajda, and I think I've been influenced by him. I worked with Andrzej Munk because we were friends and he asked me, but we had different ideas about cinema. Though I'm more like Wajda and I like his work very much, you can hardly say that I imitate him. My films are quite different from his, though his *Ashes and Diamonds* is my favorite film. Among Polish talents who are unknown here in France is Wojciech Has who made a film called *The Art of Loving.*

I'm fairly dismissive of the French *nouvelle vague* directors because they've made so many third-rate films that I can't stand. But what's wonderful is that as a movement, it's completely changed French—and maybe even global—film production. I feel that films like *Breathless* and all the François Truffaut films are works of art.

I'm also very fond of American cinema, directors like Orson Welles and Elia Kazan, and films like *Baby Doll, A Face in the Crowd,* and *Viva Zapata!* I wouldn't say I have a favorite director—I like some of a director's films and not others. I also have a soft spot for American silent comedies which I don't think you could call burlesque. To my mind, Chaplin's films are very realistic. Look at the walk-on actors—they're so natural. I also like Buster Keaton and *The World of Harold Lloyd* which has instances of pure genius, like when he climbs like an alpinist over a man who's trying to extract his own tooth. These are things that you dream and read about as a child. A real man climbing over a man twice his height—it's hilarious! You know, I don't laugh very often at the cinema. If I see something I like, I usually just laugh silently. But that Harold Lloyd film had me rolling in fits of laughter.

I have access to everything I need when I'm filming in Poland. Censorship isn't really an issue there. It's only relevant once a film is finished, but is rarely enforced. In order to make a film, a script has to be shown to a commission whose members meet once or twice a week. Each member receives the script two or three weeks before the meeting where they decide if the film can be made. There are eight production groups in Poland and I'm a member of the Kamera Group. When I have an idea, I submit it to my group leader. If he likes it, he'll ask me to develop it into a script that can be presented to the commission. If the commission rejects it, I'm not able to make the film. The commission deals only with feature films—for shorts it's different because they're less expensive and fewer people are involved. My teacher was responsible for my work and gave his approval for the two or three films I made at the Lodz Film Academy. For *Mammals* I worked with an independent production group that made shorts and that was able to make certain decisions without consulting the authorities.

In Poland I've been accused of "individualistic pessimism." Maybe this has something to do with my personality because I'm a mischievous person. But I can't say that every single critic is against me because most of them have helped a lot. Though critics are important in Poland, it's not like here in France where they can influence audiences and seriously affect a film's reception. At home the authorities support the critics, and a film director—or the group to which he belongs—would encounter serious problems if, for example, his film was labeled as reactionary by one or more official newspapers which are the mouth-pieces of the party. But it never happens.

I Made This Film for Myself

PHILIPPE HAUDIQUET/1966

H: *Up to now you have produced both shorts and features. Is there any particular reason for this?*

P: It's the subject matter of a film that dictates a particular format. It also depends on the circumstances surrounding the project. Lots of my most cherished ideas have come to nothing because I haven't been able to interest any producers in them. It really doesn't matter how long or short a film is. What's essential is that the subject matter corresponds with both the filmmaker's tastes and tendencies, and the producer's interests.

H: *What inspired you to make* Repulsion?

P: As a director I'm capable of making nice little comedies as well as more serious films. After *Knife in the Water*, the first full-length film I made in Poland—one that uses a holiday atmosphere tinged with a generous amount of irony—French critics saw me as a nice and reassuring young man. *Repulsion* hits at a gut level, so I don't think they'll be able to label me in the same way now.

H: *Is the film based on a novel?*

P: No, it's an original screenplay. The starting point was someone I know who resembles Carole, the Catherine Deneuve character. I tried to imagine what her impulses and fears were. The film could never have

From *Les lettres françaises*, 13 January 1966. Reprinted by permission of Philippe Haudiquet. Translated by Paul Cronin and Jerica Kraljic.

been set in a town like Warsaw where there aren't very many neurotics and where the isolation isn't too hard to handle. The story could only have worked in a city like Paris or London. If I'd filmed it in Poland, I would have found a place with tough working conditions where life can be pretty miserable, perhaps a working class area in Silesia where there are a lot of registered cases of mental illness. Deneuve's solitude was essential to the development of her disease.

Gérard Brach and I wrote the script together in Paris which is where the film was originally set. While writing we sometimes found ourselves in a rather strange state of mind—we needed to breath fresh air. From our tenth-floor apartment we were inspired by the liveliness of what was happening outside, including the sound of church bells. We realized they were ringing regularly in the backyard of a convent which we could see and where nuns were playing with a ball. We felt it was important to show what was happening outside Carole's apartment as a counterpoint to her story, for example the buskers I came across in London.

H: *Does the pathological phenomenon you describe correspond to an actual mental illness?*
P: Yes, the illness described really exists—it's called "schizophrenia homicide." But I'm not very interested in whether Carole's disorder stems from her childhood, and contrary to some French critics, I didn't set out to make a Freudian film. I just stuck to describing someone whose motives are sometimes difficult to fathom.

H: *It's been said of the film that only the title is truthful. What's your response to that?*
P: Everything in the film is truthful. When Carole finds herself in a strange situation, I always wanted to show her universe—as I imagined it—with as much realism and truthfulness as possible. I think I know my job pretty well. If every scene is controlled, every movement planned, every gesture directed, there's nothing but contrivance. I shot *Repulsion* in a way that felt right to me. The film taught me a lesson about just how far one can go with realism.

To express Carole's mental universe I employed all kinds of clichés. I love cinema, especially its magical elements, but this wasn't a subject that lent itself easily to the medium. I wanted to bring off something that was artistic and not just technical. I made this film for myself.

H: *Did you encounter any particular problems during production?*
P: *Repulsion* was difficult to shoot, mainly for technical reasons. I had a set built with a ceiling but it was very uncomfortable because we were filming during the summer and the studio was very hot. I was very careful about representing reality and we spent a lot of time on the details that would conjure up the right atmosphere. As for Catherine Deneuve, she is very good in the film even though she was nervous and tired. Being constantly on screen gave her no time to relax.

H: *There is very little music in the movie.*
P: The soundtracks to my films have always been very important to me, though music is never over-powering and other sounds and noises often play meaningful roles. *Repulsion* is no exception to this rule. My interest in realism is such that I would make "scented" films if I could. Not by spraying perfume all over the place—which would be ridiculous— but by some as yet un-invented method that could realistically create the illusion. What are we actually looking at on the cinema screen? Shadows and reflections. If we're so impressed by just images, our reaction to smells would probably be quite extraordinary. Think about the smells in wine cellars or in Parisian cafés. I think there's much in cinema that has yet to astonish us.

H: *There are often two or three characters in your films, and* Repulsion *is no exception. Can you explain why?*
P: What always interested me in my favorite films were the relationships between people. The fewer characters there are, the more profound and complex those relationships can be. When I was a child and went to the cinema, the scenes with a lot of characters irritated me. I remember liking *Robin Hood* with Errol Flynn—I must have seen it ten times. But it wasn't the elaborate battle scenes between the Normans and the Saxons that I found entertaining, rather the fight on a tree trunk between Robin Hood and I forget who. If I ever make a film about a revolution, I wouldn't have scenes with hoards of people. I would concentrate on characters like Lenin and Robespierre.

H: *Have you made any films since* Repulsion?

P: *Cul-de-sac*, which I'd been thinking about doing for a few years. I'm pretty stubborn and the film I finally made this summer is based on the first draft of the script. I'm happy to say that nothing was changed.

It was an exhausting shoot. We were on a small island of about a hundred and fifty people and access was difficult because of floods. The weather was terrible, the food was disgusting, and the actors turned out to be very difficult and aloof. I've never had such bad working relationships with actors, and at the end of the shoot no-one could stand each other. I'm never happy at the end of a film's production because it's difficult to see what's really been achieved. It's only much later that you're able to judge the end result. I hope it turns out OK.

H: *You've just signed a contract with the American producer Martin Ransohoff. What film will you be making with him?*

P: *The Fearless Vampire Killers*, a period comedy set in Transylvania and starring Jack MacGowan. I wrote the scenario with Gérard Brach. I just spent two days in Hollywood talking the film over with Ransohoff and I've already found the locations on the Austro-Italian border in the Dolomites. We start filming in February.

H: *The colors of your short film* When Angels Fall *are astonishing. Do you have any plan to use similar colors again?*

P: My next film will actually be in color, in Technicolor and Panavision. I'm going to shoot it in the snow, just like I did with *Mammals*, though of course the color will be somewhat stylized.

H: *In which way?*

P: Difficult to say, as the film hasn't even been made yet. And a film is like a painting or a sculpture—it's something to be looked at, not talked about.

H: *Are there any recent films you have enjoyed?*

P: *8½*, *Pierrot le fou*, *The Hill*, and the Polish film *Identification Marks: None* by Skolimowski, which is quite extraordinary. Watching it, you can really breathe the colorless atmosphere of Lodz.

H: *Do you have any Polish projects?*

P: For a while it looked like *The Fearless Vampire Killers* could be made as a co-production in Poland. There are some wonderful landscapes over there that would have suited the story perfectly, though for financial reasons it just isn't possible. But the idea of making a new film in Poland is one I still think about.

Interview with Roman Polanski

MICHEL DELAHAYE AND
JEAN NARBONI/1969

Q: The Fearless Vampire Killers *seems set to be your most important film
to date. Have you wanted to make the film for a long time?*
A: I didn't have a clear idea of the film, but I did know it would be a
fairytale comedy about vampires and that there would be lots of snow
in it. When I think about it now, it's the snow that comes to mind first.
I'd spoken to my friends about the story when we were skiing and
thought it would be wonderful to make a film that had a sleigh going
over a mountain. Then I thought of everything else you can do with
snow. *Knife in the Water* came to me in the same way. I thought of that
film first in terms of its landscape even before coming up with the
story, specifically the water in the area of Poland where all the lakes are.
So the starting point for the film was the setting and the atmosphere.

Q: *Your films often seem to grow out of a particular setting, but can a scene
develop from a single routine or gag? An example might be in* The Fearless
Vampire Killers *where the vampire chases your character about. It's something that seems to come straight out of a burlesque routine.*
A: On that occasion the idea came first and it was only afterwards
that we built the set. The routine certainly influenced the layout of the
ground floor and the courtyard. When I write a screenplay I always take
into consideration where it's going to be filmed, but here it was crucial

From *Cahiers du Cinéma*, January 1969. © *Cahiers du Cinéma*. Reprinted by permission.
Translated by Paul Cronin and Remi Guillochon.

because we had to know exactly what the location would look like. My co-writer Gérard Brach and I did our best, but it was still quite problematic. It wasn't easy to outline the set and the designer managed to sort out all the problems only by cheating in a couple of places.

Q: *A lot of people see the film as a parody of vampire stories, but though it is very funny, you handle the genre in a rather serious way, never as parody.*
A: Parody was never my intention. I wanted to make a fairy tale, something that's frightening as well as fun, but also an adventure story. Children see the two as one and the same thing—that childish desire of wanting to be frightened without there actually being any danger, of being able to laugh at your own fears. I found this aspect very appealing, like a trip to Disneyland.

Q: *Why did you choose to play a lead role in the film? Was this your attempt to deal with your fears?*
A: It was a practical decision, one that solved several problems. I couldn't think of another actor who could play the role as well as I could. I'm not saying that I'm a better actor than anyone else, but that personally I didn't have any problems with the part. While it might have been problematic asking someone else, I didn't mind playing such a ridiculous character on screen. Many actors—especially young actors—are quite self-conscious and would never have involved themselves in something like this.

Some routines required a lot of stamina and physical strength, like falling over and sliding around, carrying the Professor on the roof, things like that. I was aware that things like this would pose certain problems and take time. What's more, the character looked a lot like me, so why not play the part? Everything fell into place, though I should point out that it's not my intention to become an actor. It was simply a challenging and entertaining job that had to be done.

Making *The Fearless Vampire Killers* was great fun for me and the whole crew. I'm not sentimental but when I see the film tears come to my eyes. It reminds me of the six wonderful months we spent together which everyone has fond memories of. I think cinema is such a wonderful profession because it's fun *and* you get paid. What could be better? It was great dressing up in those costumes, putting on those ridiculous skis and chasing after each other. Of course it was physically exhausting, but that's what the film called for.

Q: *Interestingly enough, the last sentence in your previous interview with* Cahiers du Cinéma—*after mentioning that you were making the film— was "I believe that it will be wildly funny." But in that interview you also described your general outlook and spoke of two kinds of films: those you like to make and those you like to see. We got the impression that* Rosemary's Baby—*which you must have enjoyed making—was the kind of film you like to see, and that* The Fearless Vampire Killers *falls into the category of films you like to make.*

A: I was keen to make *The Fearless Vampire Killers*, but more as if I were actually an audience member. As a filmmaker who wants to show some-thing interesting or new cinematically speaking, I made *Cul-de-sac*. But for those people who want to go to the cinema for two hours and have a good time, I made *The Fearless Vampire Killers*, even if there are other considerations behind this piece of pure entertainment: the sets, the atmosphere, maybe even my childhood memories.

Q: *There is a playfulness when it comes to the techniques you used in the film, for example the scenes with the mirror where the vampires have no reflection but the non-vampires do.*

A: But are you sure the actors without reflections weren't real vampires?

Q: *Going by the story, the distinction between vampires and non-vampires is clear. In any case, the two main characters are not vampires because they get bitten at the end and only then become vampires.*

A: That makes sense, but you do seem a little too sure of yourself. Anyway, how do you think we did the trick with the mirrors?

Q: *A Jean Cocteau-style effect: you cut to the backs of the two doubles while the actors are facing forwards.*

A: Yes, that's the idea. I tried it out in several different ways but this was the simplest. I made a hole in the set where we fixed the mirrors, moved the sets behind to the other side, and put the doubles opposite the sets. We did the same thing in the scene with the bed when I'm sitting with the gay guy. I see you're interested in technical things at *Cahiers du Cinéma*. It's a shame you don't print more about this as it's actually more straightforward than what you usually write about.

Q: *We try to write about everything. We only print what people say to us.*
A: To be honest it's been more than a year since I've held a copy of *Cahiers* in my hands—not since I left for America last April. And what bothers me—or used to bother me—is a certain bias, such as the one you have for me. Why it that?

Q: *Have you seen any other good films about vampires or witches? On the whole they're dire. Your films are something of a consolation.*
A: That reminds me, have you seen Fellini's sketch in *Spirits of the Dead*? It's fantastic, truly wonderful. This is what I like about cinema: one thing grabs your attention, then a second, and suddenly magic is in the making.

Q: *Yes, it's a great film. And the way Terence Stamp looks, he wouldn't be out of place in* The Fearless Vampire Killers.
A: Absolutely, yes.

Q: *Aside from yourself, there's another unusual actor who has cropped up in one of your films: John Cassavetes in* Rosemary's Baby. *He is wonderful because he embodies the feeling of disquiet in the film, and at the same time we actually sense his awkwardness.*
A: Yes, though he didn't really feel at ease. Maybe he's a bit too much of an Actors Studio type to play a character like that. He knows how to play himself best.

Q: *He shows a lot of inventiveness in the role.*
A: Yes, but too much. In everyday life we aren't constantly making gestures. Just once we might say something without putting a finger in our ear or scratching ourselves.

Q: *But surely those gestures are inventive and meaningful. They all add something to the disturbing side of his character.*
A: I assure you he scratches himself far too much.

Q: *His character is complex, somebody who seems content, happy and in love with his wife. But at the same time he's perpetually troubled, ill-at-ease and irritated. Everything he does in the film fits with this false side of his personality.*

A: What I like about his character—and this is something I set out to capture on film—is that he's not a particularly pleasant person. If he'd been charming and likable the audience would have been immediately suspicious of him, as this is one of the basic principles of the thriller genre. Played this way, he'd made you think he doesn't have anything to do with what's going on. We sense from the way he acts that he *might* be involved, but then quickly think "No, it would be too crude. He can't have anything to do with this."

Q: *It's the opposite of crime films where we say to ourselves that the first person to be accused can't be the guilty one. You wanted to make the most obvious suspect the guilty one.*

A: Exactly.

Q: *Yet at the same time, when Rosemary is giving birth, when he is close to her and tells her everything is okay, you hope the audience will think she's wrong about him.*

A: Yes, only I don't actually want the audience to think anything in particular. I simply want it not to be sure of what's going on. It's this uncertainty that's most compelling.

Q: *A friend said something about your film that's very perceptive. For all its excellence, it lacks a particular dimension: the director's belief in the fear he is creating.* Rosemary's Baby *is a film made by somebody who doesn't actually believe in what he is showing, unlike Hitchcock who is himself quite frightened of what his films portray.*

A: It's quite possible. To begin with I'm an atheist, so accepting what happens in the film would be going against who I am and what I believe in. Consequently, I wasn't frightened and I'm still not frightened. But I'd like to take some sort of drug that would let me forget all about this film, and then go and see it for the first time just as my friends have done. Then I'd experience a bit of the fear that other people have felt. Unfortunately, as I made the film and I don't believe in either God or in the Devil—which makes my case even worse—I'm doubly incapable of being frightened by my own creation, and that really bothers me.

The reason I decided to make *Rosemary's Baby* was simply because I adored the novel. For a filmmaker like myself it's a very seductive book and made me want to film it. This is quite normal—it's like when you want to make love to a woman even though you know she's a prostitute. I told myself I really had no choice in the matter, even though the ideas behind the story are quite foreign to me.

Q: *But you stayed completely faithful to the book?*
A: I realized that I could make the film only if I remained faithful to the novel. It all started as soon as I arrived in Hollywood and was given the proofs of the book. I was very tired after the journey—because of the time difference and so on—and said to myself I'd read the book tomorrow by the swimming pool at the hotel. But I began reading the first page whilst getting ready for bed. At first I thought they'd made a mistake because it seemed like a syrupy Doris Day number, but decided to read a bit more to see how it comes together at the end. Well, believe it or not, at four o'clock I was still lying on my bed surrounded by pages from the manuscript. I just couldn't stop. The next day I went straight to the studio and told them I was really interested in doing it, but on one condition: the story stays as it is and they don't try to improve it. That's what they always do in Hollywood—try to improve great scripts that then turn out terribly. They said the book was exactly what they wanted to do.

At the time I didn't know the studio head, Bob Evans, very well. Now he's the head of all of Paramount productions and we're very friendly. He's a very confident and decisive person and stuck to what we'd agreed. He never forced me to do anything I didn't want to. However, I still had a lot of work to do because though sticking to the novel made things easier, there were still immense problems to overcome.

Q: *Maybe the advantage of* The Fearless Vampire Killers *was that you believe in the fear you were showing on screen—in so far as it is an amusing and childish fear—and yet kept it at arm's length.*
A: With *The Fearless Vampire Killers* the audience is frightened, but it's a rather pleasant kind of fear. At the same time I have a principle, my own

philosophy if you like. When I tell you I don't believe in God or witches or vampires, this means that as far as I know they don't exist. But I'm never sure of anything. In other words, the wiser I become, the more certain I am that you can't ever be certain of anything. In fact the worst thing possible is to be absolutely certain about things. Hitler, for example, must have been convinced in the certainty of his ideas and that he was right. I don't think he did anything without believing in it, otherwise he wouldn't have done it to start with. And I think that Jean-Luc Godard believes he makes good films, but maybe they aren't that good.

Q: *Everyone has something that frightens them more than anything. What is that fear for you, and could you make a film about it?*
A: There isn't any one single fear. There are hundreds of things that I'm frightened of, including dogs that chase me. Yet I adore them and own a couple.

Q: *Were* Cul-de-sac *and* Repulsion *about things you were frightened of?*
A: I've never been frightened when making films. I know other people are terrified of those films, but for me it was fun making them. They're artificial. The razor in *Repulsion,* cutting the throat—it's all just part of my job.

Q: *But the madness?*
A: I have to admit that if I think about it, madness does frighten me. Three years ago I took some LSD, something that pulls you into a state that really is a kind of madness. It frightened me because I felt I was drowning and wasn't able to hold onto anything anymore. There's a piece of furniture over here. If I touch it I know it'll feel hard, and that the telephone will be smooth. I also know that if I flick this switch, the light will go out. But when you're in this drug-induced state anything can change at any moment. The furniture can become fluid, the telephone feels rough, maybe even hot. The light might go on when I want to switch it off and vice versa. There's just nothing to hold onto any more. You try—and fail—to focus on the little bit of reality that might still exist. I found this so frightening that it's impossible to describe. It's like when you see people in asylums shouting "Doctor, help me!" They're people who have some terrible suffering inside of them, even though physically they look at peace.

Q: *Having seen films that contain evocations of LSD trips, it strikes me as being something that can't really be filmed.*

A: You can film anything, it's just that it'll resemble LSD about as much as I look like a carrot. The closest I've seen to this kind of reality is the sequence from a film I absolutely love, *2001: A Space Odyssey*. There are also psychedelic pictures that are fairly close to certain things you see when under the influence of LSD. I thought it was just me, but almost everyone sees the same kind of spiraled rings you see on silk designs. The only difference is that nothing stays still—everything moves and transforms itself. You can have any kind of hallucination but you know it'll always be continually transforming itself into something else, without knowing if it'll ever end.

Q: *And were you frightened?*

A: You bet! Extremely frightened. Because everything's there, everything's real. I knew I'd taken LSD but at the same time thought I'd never be normal again because it's so powerful and really does things to your head. It's as if you had an extraordinary computer in your head—an electronic marvel—and you've wedged a big screw-driver in there which has short-circuited the whole thing. That's what happens to your brain.

But how did you come to ask me a question about madness? Ah, yes: fear. Well, that's just it. Being mad is frightening because you know it's happening to you. All your life, thanks to your senses, you learn what reality is, at least as much as we can understand it. In any case, you learn to trust certain things, and even if you can't know absolutely everything, this gives you a basis upon which you're able to accept other certainties. Yet these are the same certainties you lose with LSD. Normally you can be sure of sitting down in a chair, but if you no longer have this assurance and suddenly sit down in an immense void, everything becomes quite harrowing. I said earlier you mustn't ever be certain of anything. But of course without any certainties at all, it just wouldn't be possible to exist.

Q: *We sense from your films your desire to link fear with pleasure, and to do this you use principally female characters. Whether it be Deneuve, Dorléac, Sharon Tate, or Mia Farrow, it seems you want to show women being pleasured, tortured, and terrified.*

A: Maybe it's just because it's easier to frighten a woman than a man. Or maybe fear is a feminine characteristic. It's feminine for a woman to be frightened—as it is for a man, in fact—though a man will try to cover up his fear. But actually everyone likes to be frightened, something that's most obvious with children. A strange thing is that if you look at the reactions of the one who frightens and the one who is being frightened, they actually resemble one another. I don't know exactly why—these are probably very basic instincts, but that's the way it is. In short, we like to be frightened, and the proof is that people pay to see certain films in the cinema.

Q: *But we get the impression that the Mia Farrow character in* Rosemary's Baby *has no such wish to be frightened. She only wants to be with her husband and child.*
A: It's not fear she feels exactly, it's anxiety, and she's not afraid for herself but rather for her child. So now we move into a different realm as another instinct comes into play: people like to be frightened without there being any danger. It's the third time I've said this now. At that point—and we see this in *The Fearless Vampire Killers*—we realize that fear is actually quite close to humor, which effectively means laughing about someone's misfortune, including our own. All fear that isn't accompanied by real danger ought to make you laugh once it's passed.

Q: *The first time the vampire appears in* The Fearless Vampire Killers *you let out a piercing scream which punctures the rising tension. This allows the viewers to laugh a little and let their feelings mix together.*
A: Precisely, otherwise the film would have taken a direction into drama which I didn't want.

Q: *But you risk confusing the audience when fear is combined with too much humor. Look at* Cul-de-sac *which in France, at least, was not a success.*
A: That's because people are used to specific genres and the different conventions that define them, and if you break those rules audiences aren't happy. If you absolutely have to break them, it has to be done gently. It's the same thing in fashion. When mini-skirts first appeared they were considered shocking, even repugnant—especially here where

the French ethos held out for a long time against that kind of thing.
But now they're accepted. Look at Truffaut's *Shoot the Piano Player*
which mixes different categories and rules. For sophisticated audiences
it was a real pleasure, and that's why the film—which I adore—had an
atrocious run in France.

Q: *You had a lot of problems with* The Fearless Vampire Killers *in the
United States. At first you weren't even given final cut for the American version.*
A: Before making the film the producer told me he'd reserved the
final cut in the United States market for himself. He said he knew the
American public better than I did and that he could help the film's
release by making necessary minor changes. At the time I assumed I
was dealing with someone honest, unpretentious, and even artistic.
After all, this was the image he projected of himself with his baggy
trousers and dirty sweatshirt. But it didn't take me long to realize he
was a hypocrite in disguise. In fact he's done this with every director
he's worked with. He lets them make their films the way they want
while he's wrapped up in the business side of things. But he's always
certain he could actually be doing a much better job than them—even
with one hand tied behind his back—if he weren't for the business side
of things he's busy with. It was only near the end of the production
that he took over the film and changed it to match his own ideas. The
whole thing taught me a good lesson.

Q: *What reasons did he give for changing the film?*
A: In the end he didn't give any reasons, he was just directing his
revenge against someone who'd disagreed with him. He was absolutely
intent on spoiling the film and cut twenty minutes, then re-dubbed it
from start to finish, including my voice and Jack MacGowran's. Then,
because the film had become incomprehensible after being cut so
much, he added a twenty-minute cartoon prologue to explain all the
gags in advance. When I saw his version, I thought it was a joke. I was
convinced that MGM would never release the film in such a state, but it
was no joke! I thought about taking my name off the credits but discovered my contract didn't allow this, so all I could do was tell the press I'd
disowned the project, though apparently I didn't even have the right to
do that. The producer phoned me to say, "We've got enough money to

bury you!" I told him, "Go ahead!" and I carried on doing what I could, which is to say very little.

I asked him if he would look at my version of the film but he wouldn't even consider it. And that wasn't all: he blocked the film's release in London where my version could be legitimately released as I had final cut in Europe. He claimed that if it were successful there it would completely discredit his own version, so the film was never released in England. In any case, he eventually proved himself wrong because when the box office figures arrived in Hollywood, it was clear that the film had been a great success all around the world in its original version, while the receipts in the United States were lower than anywhere else.

Q: *Going back to* Rosemary's Baby, *you mentioned earlier that you remained faithful to the novel. We'd like to know if the name of Roman Castevet—an unusual hybrid that suggests your name and Cassavetes'— comes from the book, or is it your invention? It can't be there by accident.*
A: It comes from the book. The name is an anagram of "Steven Marcato," and if there are any similarities it's purely coincidental. But with regards to "Roman" I suspect that the writer, Ira Levin, wanted to make some allusion to *Repulsion.* Maybe he borrowed some atmospheric motifs and, notably, what actually happens in the apartment. I'm not sure about all of this. I did ask Levin about it all and he categorically denied it. So you see that sometimes I too behave like a critic and ask people why they do what they do.

Q: *In your first interview with us—which deals with* Repulsion—*you talked about the technical aspects of the film, saying they were something of a challenge. Did you work in the same vein when making* Rosemary's Baby?
A: With *Rosemary's Baby* it was primarily the adaptation that was the issue because it was the first time I'd turned a novel into a film. As I said earlier, absolute faithfulness to the book was the most important thing to me. If you really like a book, nothing can be more disappointing to find that the film version is completely different. I wanted to keep not only the novel's spirit and atmosphere, but also the locations and characters. The problem was that the first draft of the script was 270 pages long and the film might have lasted four or five hours. It proved to be much more difficult reducing it to 160 or 170 pages and keeping

everything in than to re-write from scratch, something that took me several months. But I did shoot the film staying true to my word.

These days I have less of a feeling that I'm doing anything new. *Repulsion* was my second film, and maybe since then I've become older and more cunning. When I made *The Fearless Vampire Killers* I hadn't made a film in Hollywood before, but I treated it just like any other job that has to be done. I don't have the same kind of enthusiasm I used to. I don't mean that I'm blasé, simply that it's not as it used to be. Even during a film's preview or premiere, when everyone else is anxious, I'm quite calm. I know that what I've done is as good as I could possibly make it.

It reminds me of the story of the bull. One day a young bull notices a group of cows and says to his father, "Papa! Papa! Let's get over there quickly and give one of them a kiss!" The father looks at him and replies, "No, let's do it slowly and kiss them all." I think I'm becoming the father bull. I've asked myself where this feeling comes from but don't have any answers. Sometimes I think it's a shame because these days I find what I do less enjoyable, but perhaps it's simply that I'm becoming more secure in my work and that I don't set out to shock anymore. It might be this certainty that gives me a different kind of approach to my work, but I couldn't say for sure what really motivates me.

Q: *Jacques Demy says he has a lot of admiration for the way Hitchcock is able to bring his own personal signature to his work, something very few film-makers are able to do. But he added that this can be dangerous because it can lead to a kind of senility and rigidity.*

A: Basically there's something a little off-putting about that. I don't know if it's senility, but I do observe a phenomenon in older filmmakers that's quite irritating, almost obscene. It happens to certain artists who realize that everything going on around them is changing and moving further away from what they're doing. It basically means they feel contempt for everything, and soon enough say to themselves, "Aha! They think that I can't do the same thing? Well, I'll show them!" So they end up doing somersaults which, for them, is quite undignified. I think Hitchcock has arrived at this point, maybe Chaplin too, though ultimately I don't really know. But something odd always happens to older artists. Apart from people like Picasso or Stravinsky who've effectively remained young, most of them become so sure of themselves and are so capable of doing exactly what they want that they're unable to stay young at heart. Then suddenly they do something that's really annoying. This is especially true when it comes to filmmakers.

Q: *Your liking for precision and perfection has allowed you to devote all your energy to very specific areas. Though your films are "unreal," you seem to stick closely to reality. In* Rosemary's Baby *for example, the two neighbors are these prosaic and almost grotesque characters, but at the same time are very funny. Their voices are also very stylized—the man sounds almost like Mister Magoo.*
A: But Mister Magoo *is* a realistic character. He's a cartoon version of a certain kind of American who really exists and who you can meet in the lobby of a Hilton or in an airport falling asleep while waiting for his wife. Mr. Castavet is a good example and it makes me happy that you thought of Mister Magoo, because to me it means the character is, essentially, realistic.

Q: *The Castavet couple play the same sort of role as the Professor and his pupil in* The Fearless Vampire Killers, *namely to forge a link with all that is horrific and at the same time distract us from the horror.*
A: The difference is that in *Rosemary's Baby* these characters themselves embody the horror of the situation, and it's precisely because of this that we had to disguise them as ordinary characters. She's a midwest type who still speaks with an accent that doesn't seem authentic, though this is because I asked the actress to exaggerate it for the role. The man was meant to speak with a New York accent as this is where he's meant to be from. Unfortunately the actor's Southern accent of origin resurfaces from time to time.

Q: *This concern with accents confirms your perfectionist ideals, something we come across all too rarely.*
A: I'm so self-conscious that I'd never have attempted a film like this if I wasn't completely sure of my own abilities. Moving away from my previous work meant I could tackle the challenges a film like this threw at me. Having said that, I don't think it's such an achievement to concentrate on the little details. In fact, it would be wrong not to do so.

Q: *I very much admired the way that certain things were worked into* The Fearless Vampire Killers, *even if most people find them quite unnecessary, especially in a "fantasy" film. It has an almost documentary style when it comes to the Orthodox Jews of Eastern Europe.*

A: I'm sure that even today in some Orthodox neighborhoods in America, women shave their heads and wear wigs without anyone knowing. I say this without really being certain—it's just my intuition. In any case, it's no chore to work through things like this. Actually it's quite pleasant and very amusing, especially when you do it in a film where nobody expects to find the least bit of realism. It means I get to do some interesting and amusing work, while at the same time giving the public more than it bargained for. It's good, no? And honest too.

The more "fantastic" you are, the more realistic you become. That's why Kafka is so brilliant. He describes the most unlikely things with such realism that you're completely taken in by them, and from time to time you turn back the pages to read things again and check what happened. Every now and then you have to put the book down and say to yourself, "Is this really possible? No, it just can't be." It all stems from the fact that Kafka places himself so close to reality that you can't escape it, but at the same time he removes you from reality and you end up not knowing where you are. This is why it was a big mistake for Orson Welles—even though he'll always be my master—to make his version of Kafka's *The Trial* so grandiose, as this is the exact opposite of what Kafka does with his writing. We ended up with a very interesting Welles but a mediocre Kafka.

You see, only a certain humility or—better still—modesty is needed to understand a book. When you choose to adapt a novel you find truly interesting, it's vital that you know what you're committing yourself to. You have to submit yourself completely to the text. Unless, that is, you choose a story you're not really interested in, one that only serves as a pretext to constructing something completely different on screen. Shakespeare started with mediocre stories and turned them into something extraordinary.

Q: *In your last interview you talked about Skolimowski. Have you seen his latest films?*

A: I haven't seen *Hands Up* for the simple reason that absolutely no-one has either. There haven't even been private projections—it just isn't

allowed. And if Skolimowski had shown it to someone he would have
been shot or hung by his toes. But I have seen his film *The Departure*
which I found charming, if a bit forced and boring, a bit poetic and pretentious. But it's still pleasant to watch. Anyway, it must have been a
tour-de-force for him to make the film with that budget in Belgium. I still
think his best work is *Identification Marks: None.*

Q: *And* Barrier*?*
A: I've seen *Barrier* and out of all of Skolimowski's films it's the one I
like the least. It really bothers me when I get the feeling that someone's
trying to impress me. Incidentally, this is the kind of thing that most
French films are doing now. This tendency of showing things in the
most gimmicky way has moved from short films to full-length features.

Q: *Can you really generalize like that? Of course there are a lot of bad films
like this, but surely not everything.*
A: There are still too many! Remember there's no art without sincerity, and even very sophisticated or completely twisted filmmakers give
a certain value to what they do because of their sincerity.

Q: *Don't you think that Skolimowski and Godard are sincere?*
A: I don't know. Maybe, yes. Anyway, sincerity isn't enough. As for
Skolimowski, I don't think he's being sincere in *Barrier*. It's very hard for
me to talk about him because he's a dear and talented friend. But you
did ask me, and questions are there to be answered.
    Anyway, I hope Skolimowski will get rid of what I don't like in his
films because I honestly think they're a real handicap to him. There are
two things I don't like about his films. I've already talked a bit about the
first one: his need to impress people and show something different no
matter what. He's good at publicity and even talks about things before
he does them: "I'll do some five or even eight minute shots." You can
see this in his second film. But anyone with a minimum of intelligence
and technical skill could do the same. I might just as well say, "Let's
make a film in a single shot!" But what's the point? Hitchcock did it
with *Rope* which, in my opinion, is a completely unbearable film. It's
boring because the camera has to maneuver around everything instead
of cutting, and has to show everything all the time instead of only when

there's actually something that needs to be seen. The result is a film full of totally bewildering effects. You just don't know where you are or where you're going, and you certainly don't understand anything about the apartment where this is taking place. All for good reason: each reel begins and ends with shot of a wall or a partition or something that closes up the space. But when a shot starts by staring at a wall you automatically say to yourself there must be something behind the wall that can't be seen. Then, unfortunately, you realize it was simply a wall or someone's back or a box—this chest they're carting around. And then it starts all over again: a wall followed by another wall. It's awful! It was after seeing *Rope* that I actually began to wonder if Hitchcock really was a great director. Before then I was a great fan of his work, right up until *Rear Window* which I saw four or five times.

But I don't want to talk about Hitchcock. I really don't care about him. I prefer talking about Skolimowski. His second defect is his kind of "poetic" playfulness. I'm not talking about real poetry that has nothing to do with playfulness and that emerges only out of sincerity. I'm talking about the kind of posturing and affectation you see with children. Instead of simply asking for some candy, they whine about it. That's what annoys me, you know? You can see this in Skolimowski's dialogue which, unfortunately, isn't easy to understand. When I say unfortunately, I actually mean fortunately, because all too often his dialogue is flowing with this kind of juvenile whining.

I continue to believe wholeheartedly in his talent and hope and feel that the film he's making now will do him justice. The script isn't his own and he isn't acting in it, a combination that might be good for the film. I'm not saying he's a bad actor. On the contrary, he showed himself to be one of the finest Polish actors with *Identification Marks: None* and *Walkover*. He speaks naturally, he doesn't show off, he's direct and unpretentious. If only he could make more films like *Identification Marks: None* it would be wonderful.

Q: *Do you have any projects in mind right now?*
A: I have two projects with Paramount but I don't know which one I'll do first.

One of them is a Western which Ivan Moffat is working on. It takes place in 1946 and is a slice of American history that hasn't ever been filmed but about which there's a lot of literature. The other is a science-fiction book that the author is writing at the moment and which I've read only half of. I'm waiting impatiently for the second half. I won't tell you the name of the author because I'm not committed to it yet. For the time being I'm just very interested, but I do think it'll be a good project.

Q: *Before we finish is there anything you'd like to add?*
A: There are definitely lots of things I'd like to talk about but it's difficult to express yourself when you're asked in that way. It's like when someone asks, "So! Give me an example!" But since we've mentioned science-fiction, there's only one film that I really liked on that subject, *2001: A Space Odyssey*. There was also *Village of the Damned* fairly recently, a very low budget British film which wasn't that well made but had something extraordinary about it. It could have been a major film.

I'm surprised *2001* wasn't as appreciated in France as it was in America. I think the French are a bit behind. Maybe they just ignore too many things, not only when it comes to technology but also on the level of certain scientific discoveries. And if these ideas aren't completely ignored then they're treated with some hostility. I meet lots of people who find the beginning of *2001* ridiculous or excessive, even though it's based on the evolutionary theory of human beings having originated in Africa, a discovery that's ten or twenty years old but which seems to have been totally overlooked in France. When I discuss it with people here—even intelligent well-informed people—I realize that when it comes to evolution they've read no wider than Darwin. And I've also found that the same people react with some hostility to Desmond Morris's *The Naked Ape*. I've the impression the book disturbs them.

Q: *It could be that French thinking has always stayed "scientific" in the nineteenth-century meaning of the word. It's not surprising that science-fiction isn't well received here.*
A: It surprises me all the same. As we see in *2001*, science and imagination are constantly bouncing off each other in extremely precise ways. There's no other film where the fantasy elements are based on such rigorous documentation. I'm fascinated by the ape sequence and the way Kubrick shows the link between the development of intelligence and the handling of objects. It's the presence of the tool—with

which the ape learns how to kill—and the chance discovery of its capabilities that lies at the origin of the evolution of our nervous system and consequently the "creation" of our brain. What made us who we are today is the fact that we used to be aggressive apes who had to kill and defend our territory.

Q: *On the subject of* Cul-de-sac, *do you think the film shocks or disconcerts people?*
A: I think so, yes. For example, in New York—where unfortunately the film was released in a version with ten minutes cut out—the critics read all kinds of things into it: homosexuality, necrophilia, sadism, masochism. I can't remember all the "isms" they listed. You really got the impression that a new dictionary had been written in New York. So it didn't shock only the audience, but also the critics.

Q: *Do you plan to make a film one day that really shocks?*
A: I can't say in advance, as what's shocking for other people might not be for me. Needless to say, I won't know at the time if a film is really in the same vein as *Cul-de-sac*. Anyway, the starting point of that film was freedom of expression. It was sort of like, "Let's go—you can do what you want!" Today I'm aware of these same freedoms but in a different way. I've also become more conscientious and would like to be more constructive. I don't mean I wasn't saying anything with *Cul-de-sac* because I feel the film has a very human element to it, but I want to be a bit more positive now. What I'd really like to do, for example, is make a full-length version of my short *Two Men and a Wardrobe*. But it's much easier to express an abstract idea in a short film. It has to be a very strong idea to keep people's attention for two hours, though it's possible to get around this problem by dealing with something other than the main idea of the story. Faulkner's work, for example, is like this. It might seem ridiculous to say so, but his *Sanctuary* expresses the same kind of thing that *Two Men and a Wardrobe* does. It speaks of the intolerance and stupidity of society.

Q: *Would you like to make a film based on one of his books?*
A: I'd love to, but they're so powerful and, above all, textual. It makes them extraordinary difficult to film.

Interview with Roman Polanski

MICHEL CIMENT, MICHEL PEREZ,
AND ROGER TAILLEUR/1969

Q: *Where did you get the idea for* Rosemary's Baby?
A: The producer Bill Castle, who works for Paramount, bought the
rights. Then Bob Evans, a Paramount executive, called and said he
had two projects for me. He knows I love skiing and that I wanted
to make a film where we'd get to ski, and he had a screenplay
called *Downhill Racer.* I went to see him and he told me about the
novel *Rosemary's Baby* instead which was about to be published. I
went back to my hotel. I was very tired because of jet-lag and wanted
to go to bed so I could start reading it the next day, but I was curious
to see what the script was about so I looked at the first page, and it
seemed to be a kind of ridiculous Doris Day comedy. Evans must
have made a mistake! But I read on, and at four in the morning was
still reading.

The next day Evans was waiting for me at the studio, delighted to
know that I'd been won over by the script. I told him I wanted to make
the film so long as Paramount didn't make any "improvements" to the
story. He said that it was exactly what he wanted to do and called Bill
Castle, who at the time I didn't know personally. Castle is a low-budget
film producer who's made 125 films as director and producer. They
asked me which screenwriter I wanted and I said I'd try to write it
myself, seeing at the end of the week whether it was working out

---

From *Positif,* February 1969. Permission granted by Michel Ciment. Translated by
Paul Cronin and Remi Guillochon.

or not. I went back to London and began writing. I was very enthusiastic and after three weeks had a finished script of 260 pages. Then I
returned to Hollywood to start trimming it down.

Q: *Is this the first time you have adapted a novel for a film?*
A: Yes, and it's very faithful to the original. The book was very
seductive for a filmmaker and I wanted to be faithful to it. I also knew
it would be a best-seller and had remembered that when I went to the
cinema to see a film adapted from a book that I'd enjoyed, I usually
discovered they were actually telling a completely different story.
When I was fourteen I often thought about making a film from a
book that I was reading.

Q: *Did you make the film because you wanted to rediscover the pleasure
of reading?*
A: I don't know if that's what it was. If you're a painter and
something is described to you, then you want to draw it. If you're an
actor and you see someone interesting, you want to imitate him. If
you're a filmmaker and you read a good book, you want to turn it
into a film. These are very primitive desires. It's not about recreating
the pleasure of reading. I love reading, but this is a different type of
enjoyment.

Q: *In spite of your faithfulness, you did change some details at the end
of the story.*
A: The book's ending was a bit disappointing and I felt it dragged.
For me it was a big mistake to describe what the child looks like. Even
if a description is quite literal in a book, it still leaves a lot to the
imagination. But of course it's not the same in a film. If you show a
rabbit, it's most definitely a rabbit, and a horse is a horse. I know from
experience that when you go to the cinema to see a science-fiction
film, sometimes you shudder with suspense as you're sitting there
sweating, knowing there's a complete mystery being played out in
front of you. Finally the moment comes when "they" arrive in their
flying saucers. The most frightening thing is when the door opens and
the aliens appear. Then the fun begins.

Q: *But the ending of the film remains somewhat ambiguous. The audience might feel that the whole story about witchcraft is actually nothing more than Rosemary's fantasy.*

A: All the better then. I don't remember which philosopher it was who said "You must be obscure." It's a principle of drama. If you want to make a book or film interesting, you can't be too explicit, otherwise it's already digested for the audience. Look at Walt Disney's films where there's no ambiguity at all.

Q: *Throughout the film it's possible to believe that Rosemary is trying to escape the colorless reality of her world, to find something more real: the world of witches, something closer to nature than this world of consumerism.*

A: That's a very twisted idea. *Positif* is starting to resemble *Cahiers du Cinéma*!

Q: *And furthermore, at the point when she rejoins the witches' gathering, we move to another level: we go inside her head and realize she's mad.*

A: I don't know about that. I'm just the filmmaker.

Q: *Did you research witchcraft for the film?*

A: Very little, though there are actually a lot of witches around. In England there are 30,000 registered witches and by chance I got to know a King and a Queen witch in London two years before making the film. It was before I started *The Fearless Vampire Killers*. My wife, Sharon Tate, was making a film in England, and I was interviewed by television for a weekly discussion program. Among the other guests were these two witches in their garb. The forty-year old King was quite ugly and the Queen wasn't much better looking. They were asked questions about their rituals and ceremonial clothes. A writer made fun of them but they didn't react, and rather philosophically said to him, "You wouldn't be able to be a witch because you don't have any sympathy for other people." "Well, who could be a witch?" he asked. The guy turned toward me and said, "Him." I was very surprised. They were "good" witches, and as you know the witches in *Rosemary's Baby* are evil.

"Good" witches want to make people happy—it's an anti-religion. In principle the genesis of witchcraft is a counter religion to Catholicism. That's why most of their symbols are inverted Catholic symbols: the cross, the black mass. It's a kind of mockery. Anyway, the next day Sharon told me the same witches were in the studio with her because the film she was making was about witchcraft. They had been invited to the studio for publicity reasons and to give their advice. There were some journalists and photographers there who asked them to demonstrate their rituals, so the two of them started to do a dance with knifes and took their clothes off.

Q: *Is this what made you want to direct a film about witches?*
A: No, I never wanted to make a film about witches. *Rosemary's Baby* is not about witches.

Q: *What was the reaction to the film from Catholics in the United States?*
A: The official reaction was, unsurprisingly, not very warm. Actually, I don't know if it's fair to say "unsurprisingly" as I'd thought they might have been a little more intelligent about it. They gave it an 'X' rating which is the absolute worst—it's given to very few films. Although I really liked the book, what annoyed me when I was writing the screenplay was the deist aspect to the story. By accepting that the Devil exists, which is absolutely essential in this context, you also have to accept that God exists.

Q: *And what was the witches' response?*
A: I don't know what they thought of the film, but there was certainly a good turn-out. It's been an enormous success and I know that a good number of Catholics went to see it. But the staunch Catholics railed against the film, especially in the South where the local censor banned it in lots of small towns, for example Salem—and that's meant to be a witches' town! Of course it caused an outcry in America. Every newspaper there has a selection of letters to the editor, something I find very healthy. Some of them exclaimed that they shouldn't be told what they can and cannot go to see, but others said, "I haven't seen *Rosemary's Baby* and don't want to see it, and I'm grateful to our town sheriff who has saved us from this muck. We're

already so indoctrinated with communism that we can't see the harm being done to our youngsters. It's a great shame that the film has already been screened in other towns."

Q: *How do you explain the success of the film in America?*
A: Hey, it's a good film! And certain things worked in our favor, like the book already being a bestseller. It was a pre-sold commodity and Mia Farrow is in it. I saw the film in Los Angeles where 90 percent of the public is between eighteen and thirty. Successful films in America can be divided into two categories: films that young people—those from sixteen to thirty-five—go to see, and those that families go to. Old people and children go to see *The Sound of Music*, something that people of my age generally aren't interested in.

Q: *Have all your films been successful?*
A: Not like *Rosemary's Baby*. Scandal always helps with commerce, though not all films that set out to shock are necessarily successful. Some people say the film's success is because of the sex, but I don't feel there's actually that much sex in it. In America there are cinemas showing porno films because there's no censorship of those kinds of things. In Los Angeles there's a cinema on Santa Monica Boulevard called The Paris, and after *Rosemary's Baby*—which has the tagline, "Pray for Rosemary's baby"—they played a film called *Rosemary's Beaver*. Their tagline was "Pray for Rosemary's pussy."

Q: *So you didn't manage to attract the kind of people who went to see, for example, Hitchcock's films of the 1940s?*
A: That public simply doesn't exist any more.

Q: *Although you explore them differently, the themes of your films are similar to those in Hitchcock's* Suspicion *or* Notorious *with all those personality splits and suspicions.*
A: I really don't know about that.

Q: *What was it like working with Mia Farrow?*
A: Great. She's very conscientious, hard-working and receptive, like blotting paper. She's wonderfully natural, which at the start was the

cause of a misunderstanding. I didn't say anything to her for several days while I was directing the other actors, so she thought that maybe it wasn't working out. But on the contrary, it was going so well there really was nothing more to tell her. I said, "Wait until there are some more dramatic scenes, then we'll need to do some work together." When it came to the more gut-wrenching moments, I had to push her a little bit, but generally she was wonderful.

Q: *And what about John Cassavetes? What's it like to direct a filmmaker?*
A: He's not a filmmaker—he's made some films, that's all. Anyone could take a camera and do what he did with *Shadows*. I haven't seen *Faces*. It's more the people he surrounds himself with who actually make the films. When he became a filmmaker he got the chance to work within the studio system and showed he was completely incapable of doing so, whatever he might say about it being Hollywood's fault. I went to Hollywood and it worked OK for me. He's a very inconsistent actor and we had to clean up his performance a great deal in the editing.

Q: *How much control do you have during the editing process?*
A: I do everything at all times. I had a wonderful editor who helped me a great deal called Sam O'Steen who did *The Graduate*, a film no one likes in France. They think it's facile, but I think you have to live in the United States to appreciate it. Of course things that seem accomplished can also appear mediocre to an American. Have you seen *2001: A Space Odyssey*? It's great, but people don't seem to like it here. How much longer does it seem than *Rosemary's Baby*? Half an hour? Actually *2001* is 2 hours 19 minutes, and *Rosemary's Baby* is 2 hours 16 minutes. There's only three minutes difference between them.

Q: *With* Rosemary's Baby, *you've created a fantasy story which also contains a very down-to-earth reality. The characters are actually very ordinary, like the heroine in Repulsion.*
A: Everything begins on a very ordinary pedestrian day-to-day level. Their strangeness comes through bit by bit.

Q: *Is there a connection between* Rosemary's Baby *and* Repulsion?
A: That really isn't very important. I'm not in the process of creating
my work as you'd furnish an apartment. There are some people who are
more interested in the creation of their artistic persona than their work
itself, like Salvador Dali.

Q: *All your films are very different?*
A: Yes, like Picasso's paintings.

Q: Repulsion *includes subjective shots, but there are none in* Rosemary's
Baby.
A: Indeed. It's a semi-subjective story. The camera is always with
Rosemary, but the film isn't told from her point of view. *Repulsion* and
Rosemary's Baby deal with different subject matters. One sets out to ana-
lyze how the mind works, the other deals with a character's behavior.

Q: *Are the dreams in the film important?*
A: Yes, I wanted to include several dream sequences.

Q: *How did you manage that?*
A: I wanted the dreams in the film to look as close as possible to my
own dreams. No one dreams in exactly the same way, but I did speak to
lots of people when thinking about these sequences and asked them
what sort of dreams they have. It turns out that our dreams are actually
quite similar. In dreams nothing is ever static—everything moves and
changes. I might be talking to you when suddenly you become the
President, even if he still looks like you. So we understand dreams in
more than one way: they aren't only about what we see but also what
we know for sure. In a dream it might appear that I'm talking to my
wife, though it might actually be my father standing in front of me.
Even if she has the appearance of my wife, I know it's really my father.
Obviously this kind of thing isn't easy to show on screen.

Q: *Did you use particular lenses and camera angles for the dream*
sequences, or was the color altered?
A: I changed the color a bit. I'm not sure why but colors in dreams
aren't very clear or vibrant—there's not much contrast. That's why most

people think they dream in black and white, which is rather silly because it's so artificial and a long way from the way the brain actually understands the world. It was only with the invention of photography that reality was depicted in black and white. Color is a difficult thing to remember. What I mean is that if you ask someone to describe something they've seen, often they'll make a mistake about the color. My wife just came in. Do you remember the color of her clothes?

Q: *Black pants and . . .*
A: And her top? Was it red, green, or white? It was beige! People say, "Ah! Today I dreamt in color," but this is only when those colors took on some dramatic importance—like blood for example. Three years ago I took LSD and noticed that certain hallucinations look a lot like dreams. You might hallucinate an animal, for example, but it doesn't last—pretty soon it changes shape and becomes something else. As with dreams, nothing is static. In *Rosemary's Baby* I tried to maintain this kind of continuity by making very few cuts. It's almost one single slow moving shot. There's also a kind of slow-motion to all dreams. And as with color, the background in a dream exists only when it has some importance and when you're looking right at it. If someone speaks to you or if you see an animal or something else, I don't know why but there's just no background to the action. Of course, in a film it's not so easy to remove the background—everything is up there on the screen. It's not really the same thing if you make it blurred, and I dropped this idea when Rosemary has her nightmare, which is actually neither a dream nor reality.

Q: *How do you see the film today?*
A: I can't see it any more! I went with my wife to see how the public responded to it and asked her, "Tell me, was there a scene in a cemetery?" I simply couldn't remember certain parts. My attention begins to drift and my brain blocks me out of the film because I've seen it so many times. If you want to ask what originally interested me in the book I can answer you, but I don't know if the film matches up to my original conception. My real interest was in bringing the book to life.

Q: *Before going to America, you said you were frightened because of*
Hollywood producers. What was your experience of working over there?
A: My experience has been a very good one, for two reasons. Bill
Castle has a lengthy career as a filmmaker—if you can call it a career,
as the films he made were never very good. He never pretended he
was making masterpieces, but he's an excellent technician who
understands filmmakers' problems and doesn't have the usual worries
other producers have. He made a constant effort to make me happy in
my work. I can't think of a better producer. The second reason is that
Bob Evans is a young guy—only thirty-eight years old and head of
Paramount. He was resolute and always believed in me, even allowing
me to go over budget which is inexcusable in Hollywood. It's thanks to
those two men that I was able to make exactly the film I wanted to.

Q: *Your experience with producer Martin Ransohoff was different though,*
wasn't it?
A: Ransohoff is a perfect example of a hypocrite. He's a philistine who
dresses himself up as an artist. He's very pretentious. In all honesty, the
man's a brute.

Q: *Not many people have seen your short film* River of Diamonds *which is*
part of the film The Beautiful Swindlers.
A: It's really not that good. It comes from an original script I wrote
with Gérard Brach, and was the first film we worked on together. It
wasn't our first screenplay collaboration as we'd already written
Cul-de-sac, though no one even wanted to read it.
    I wanted to make *River of Diamonds* in Amsterdam as a co-production.
Each segment of the film takes place in a different country and we had
a Dutch producer. Amsterdam is a town full of diamond-cutters and I
decided to do something about that. Gérard and I went to Cartier to get
some information and the shop owner was very helpful, telling us quite
a lot about swindling. This gave us a starting point for the story.

Q: *Is the film based on a true story?*
A: The starting point was a true story, but the film is long way from
the truth.

Q: *It seems to come straight out of an Amsterdam guide book.*
A: When I make a film I use what's around me. *Knife in the Water*
is a guide to the Mazury region of Poland, and *The Fearless Vampire
Killers* is the same for Transylvania. A device I try to include in my
films is like the one in the Van Eyck painting of the Arnolfini couple
with a mirror behind them. Above the mirror it says something like,
"I was there." Artists of that era wanted their audiences to be literally
inside their paintings, and they even produced work that were kind
of boxes with holes to look through so you could see the art. You've
never seen these things? It's like seeing inside a house. When I'm an
audience member I don't just want to be in the cinema but actually
right inside the film itself.

Q: *Of all your films,* Cul-de-sac *seems the most detached from reality.*
A: From a cinematic point of view it's certainly my best film. If I
went in search of cinema, just as Samuel Beckett goes in search of
theater, I would only make films like *Cul-de-sac.* Unfortunately—or
maybe fortunately—I like to amuse myself, so I also make films
like *The Fearless Vampire Killers* and *Rosemary's Baby.*

Q: *In what way is* Cul-de-sac *the kind of cinema that you enjoy making?*
A: I didn't say it was the kind of cinema I enjoy making, rather
it's the most valuable kind of film from a cinematic point of view. If
I wanted to do something relevant to what's happening today—
especially contemporary cinema—then *Cul-de-sac* is the kind of film
I'd make again. Nobody told Brach and me which direction to go in
when we sat down to write the script. We had absolutely nothing, not
even a structure for the story. All we wanted to do was get on and write
something. It's as if you give someone some brushes and a canvas, and
then tell them, "Go on, paint something." We started to create scenes
and characters who connected with the things that interested us at
the time, both in life and in the cinema. We went to see films every
day and soon the characters began to create a story for themselves. It
eventually developed into a screenplay and we went to work on the
structure by adding and cutting.

Q: *Do you make changes during shooting?*

A: Only if I can improve on what's in the script. I think the only real explanation for a three-page screenplay script is laziness. You waste far too much energy during filming if the script hasn't been worked through properly. More perspiration during maneuvers means less sweat for the real battle.

Q: *Did you stick more to the script when you made* Knife in the Water *and* Rosemary's Baby *than with* Cul-de-sac?

A: *Cul-de-sac* stayed closer to the original screenplay than *Repulsion* did. But if I feel the natural surroundings of a location are different to those in the screenplay and that taking advantage of this would bring a new perspective, I won't hesitate to change things. For *Cul-de-Sac* there was one vital thing: the tide. Though it's possible to find things like this in France, I flew in a plane around England until I'd found the right location.

Q: *Isn't* Cul-de-sac *your favorite film because it's your most "unconformist" work?*

A: Perhaps, yes. One principle I try to bring to my work is that things happen despite our expectations. If someone says something, we wait for a certain reaction. Throughout the film you might think that the gangster will kill the husband, but never the other way around. Yet that's exactly what happens.

Q: *Why has Teresa (Françoise Dorléac) married George (Donald Pleasance)?*

A: I don't want to have to say it again, but I'm only the filmmaker! If you think of your friends you'll find that many of them have beautiful wives. They won't be able to explain why they married their husbands.

Q: *Who is Teresa?*

A: A girl who wasn't doing anything with her life and who was in trouble. He even calls her a semi-prostitute, though she certainly didn't marry for money. There are a lot of girls who think they're being radical by doing things a little out of the ordinary, and everything she does—like provoking the gangsters and playing with the kid by pulling his ear—falls into the same category as her marriage.

Q: *Who is Katelbach [the character the gangsters are waiting for]?*
A: A friend of mine when I was down and out in Paris. He was really quite interesting and I liked him a great deal.

Q: *He's like Godot.*
A: But Katelbach exists—they speak to him on the phone.

Q: *Do you always make a distinction between your characters and the outside world?*
A: I don't know. The distinction intrigues me because people act in a more sincere way when they feel isolated. Let's imagine that all of a sudden this house collapses and we find ourselves trapped here for two or three months. Our true nature would be unleashed as we fight over who's going to eat the flowers over there.

Q: *You once said that the young man in* Knife in the Water *was superfluous and that the real story is about the couple.*
A: I never said he was superfluous but that the real seed of the drama is contained in the relationship between the man and woman. The third person who walks through the history of literature is merely an excuse. Those aren't my words, they come from Rilke's *Notebooks of Malte Laurids Brigge*: "What have I written? Very little. A very bad treatise on marriage. If I were to write it now I would know not to include a third person."

Q: *Are you an anarchist?*
A: Yes, it's very healthy to be anarchistic.

Q: *Jean-Daniel Simon filmed a screenplay of yours and Brach's,* The Girl Across the Way *[La Fille d'en Face].*
A: I saw the film and unfortunately it's not that good. We wrote it for English television and he made it into a feature film. But I think Simon was too literal and respectful of the screenplay and dialogue. The actor didn't get into the role and I felt he didn't really identify with the young boy. The film doesn't make much sense because of this.

Q: *Is the shot of the musicians walking backwards in the screenplay of* Repulsion?

A: Yes, but not in the first version. I came to London, saw the musicians in the road, and said to Gérard Brach, "Those buskers have to be in the film. It could be useful to hear them from the window when she's shut inside the house. It would add a bit of flavor from the outside world, as if she were in a nunnery."

Q: *We know of several psychiatrists who like* Repulsion.

A: Psychiatrists everywhere like the film. A famous Austrian professor told me that one element of the film had greatly surprised him, that the heroine hears things with a great deal more acuity than normal people. This is a recent discovery in psychiatry, that schizophrenics loose the ability to select the noises they hear, that they hear sounds we don't hear, ones we would normally eliminate. In New York a woman from Columbia University told me the film was screened several times for psychiatrists.

Q: *Is this authenticity the result of medical research you did for the film?*

A: No, it's all just intuitive. I've not read anything about it. Intuition is the sum of experience.

Q: *Does the photo we see at the beginning and end of* Repulsion *in some way represent Deneuve's jealousy for her sister?*

A: I really don't know about that. I'm just the filmmaker.

Q: *Did the idea for* Repulsion *come to you initially because you wanted to make a horror film?*

A: To be frank, yes. Even though during the film's production things changed, the initial idea was to make a horror film. I'd like to deny this but it just wouldn't be true.

Q: *Audiences were furious because at the start they sympathized with Deneuve's character but then found themselves implicated in what she was doing.*

A: They were angry to have let themselves be tricked. Audiences in France don't like this kind of thing, although it was a triumph in Germany.

Q: *The characters are always helpless at the end of your films.*
A: If you show your hero triumphant, the audience leaves satisfied. And there's nothing more sterile than the state of satisfaction.

Q: *In France there is a debate raging about films that don't use screenplays and that have amateurish acting. Amongst young filmmakers you seem to be making personal but nonetheless very professional films.*
A: The others are all amateurs. It's the same with writers. Someone might not be able to write a sentence, yet his work can still be interesting. If a young girl of thirteen describes her adventures with a dirty old man, it's interesting, even if her storytelling style is poor. But cinema isn't like a naïve picture or a primitive drawing which is always emotionally touching, no matter what. When amateurish, cinema is often very pretentious, and even young filmmakers who have the necessary technique to make decent films feel that merely telling a story isn't enough. They want to impress us by filling their films with improbable effects to make them seem as different as possible from everything else. They cut the film up, they shake the camera about and they manipulate the sound. But for what purpose? Everyone knows things like this are possible with film. But being simple—now there's a real talent. The simpler you are, the more complex you become—not superficially but in a deep way.

Q: Rosemary's Baby *is your simplest film.*
A: It's actually full of intricate camera moves, but we don't generally notice because they're relevant to the story.

Q: *There is a kind of Jewish humor that comes through in* The Fearless Vampire Killers. *How familiar are you with this?*
A: In the film there's an Eastern European culture which was desolated by the Germans and that's been killed off for good thanks to Polish Stalinism. It's the kind of thing that you can see in the work of figures like Mark Chagall and Isaac Babel, and also in certain Polish paintings. This culture, which never reappeared after the war, is part of my childhood memories. There just aren't any traditional Jews in Poland any more—it's something that exists more in America and certain districts of France.

Q: *Three of your films could be seen as horror films. Will you make a more traditional horror film one day?*

A: No, that doesn't interest me, though I do like to go to the cinema to see funny films about vampires, and even get a little frightened.

Q: *You mentioned 2001. What other recent films have interested you?*

A: I've already seen it twice. I saw *Dr. Stangelove* twice too. It's even more impressive now than it was five years ago. I like *The Graduate* and *Bonnie and Clyde*, and loved *Closely Observed Trains*.

Q: *What was it that fascinated you about 2001?*

A: Everything, especially the way the subject was approached. You can see that it's very much anchored in science and is absolutely modern in every way. The first sequence with the monkeys is a cinematic version of a theory which is only twenty years old and that's wonderfully described in a book called *African Genesis* by the American writer Robert Ardrey. Man—not modern man, I mean those who came between the ape and modern man—was a killer who used weapons, and this is what caused his brain to develop. It wasn't his developing brain that led him to pick up a bone and use it as a weapon, it was the other way round.

Q: *So is humanity dependent on warfare?*

A: No, that's a very dangerous idea. The destructive urge is one of the base instincts, like sex, and it's actually society that represses such instincts. But there are other kinds of societies on earth. Look at the way ants and bees live.

Q: *How did you interpret the ending of 2001?*

A: It's extremely ambiguous, but we're led to understand that if there is a vastly superior intelligence, then we're incapable of understanding and perceiving it. If it contributes to our development, then it might well be hidden from us. Kubrick gives this idea a cinematic form. Apart from that, what I like about the film are its technical and magical aspects. It's full of fascinating effects like the voyage into space at the end. It's a real "trip." There are people who give themselves a headache trying—and failing—to show how it really is when you take LSD. I've seen very weak efforts in other films. Without showing it directly, the film has really grasped what you see when you take LSD.

Q: *With* The Fearless Vampire Killers, *did you want to make a parody and at the same time a film with rather serious elements?*
A: I never wanted to make fun of horror films and I never wanted to make a parody either, just a comedy in the vampire genre. I wanted to tell a romantic story that was funny and frightening at the same time. These are the things we like to see when we're children. We go to the funfair, sit in the ghost train, and hope to be frightened. When we laugh and get goose-pimples at the same time it's a pleasant feeling because we know there's no real danger.

Q: *The end of* The Fearless Vampire Killers *is practically science-fiction with the vampire lying underneath the moon taking possession of the earth.*
A: The ending is even more satirical than the rest of the film. In every vampire film the vampires are always killed at the end and the Professor saves the world from this terrible plague. Here, it's the menace that wins out.

Q: *And at the end of* Rosemary's Baby *it's the monsters who are victorious.*
A: Yes, the Devil prevails.

Roman Polanski

DICK CAVETT/1971

C: *My next guest's film version of* Macbeth *is something people have been hearing and talking about for some time. It's his first film since* Rosemary's Baby *and it's been awaited with terrific interest in the film world—his first film since his life became public in a very tragic way some years back, and it's great to have him working again. His other films have been called enigmatic and macabre, and* Macbeth *is the perfect film for him to direct. It's a pleasure to welcome Roman Polanski.*

Kenneth Tynan wrote an article about Macbeth and said that they were going to fire you?

P: On every film they're trying to fire me.

C: *How many times has this happened to you?*

P: It happened virtually as many times as I've tried to direct a film.

C: *Every film?*

P: Practically. They take the film away from me, let's put it this way.

C: *How do they dare do that? Doesn't it cross their mind that nobody else is going to finish it quite the way you would have?*

P: Well, they always say, "We love the rushes, we love the dailies. What you are doing is great, but can you do it cheaper and faster?"

From *The Dick Cavett Show*, 22 December 1971. Reprinted by permission of Daphne Productions.

c: *It's always over money?*

p: Only. I think that in Tynan's article—I don't remember because it was quite a while ago that I read it—he mentioned I had exactly the same problem during the shooting of *Rosemary's Baby*. I met Otto Preminger on the Paramount lot and he asked me what I was worried about, and I told him, and he said, "But they never fire a director for going over-budget." I said, "But they've fired many directors before." And he said, "Yes, for lousy dailies, for lousy results, but never for going over-budget. They try to press you this way." And I thought back, and indeed I thought of cases when directors were replaced, and since then I'm not worried about it. And if they take it away, I can do another one. A better one, maybe.

c: *But wouldn't it kill you having a film taken away, two-thirds finished?*

p: It would have killed me some time ago, but not now. I think you become less sensitive from film to film because you know the agony of it. People think one exaggerates using such a word, but it is an agony to go through a film. Most films are done this way—most go over-budget. In fact, most enterprises go over-budget. Probably the skyscraper right behind here went over-budget because it's very difficult to foresee exactly what materials and working hours you need. Each film is a new experience, it's not even a skyscraper where you can measure the blocks of steel. Each film always turns out a bit better than I was anticipating, and to make it better costs more money.

c: *But don't you want some guarantee that two-thirds of your movie isn't going to be taken over by someone else who's going to finish it and call it Polanski's movie?*

p: The people who give money for the films are giving money because of me. I managed through years of struggle to create this situation that is quite convenient for me, that people think my movies are going to be a success. They are interested only in the profits of it, so in a sense they buy me as a director. They buy me, not Shakespeare. When I said I wanted to do Shakespeare, they thought it was a disease. They thought I was crazy. My own agent said, "What are you doing to me?"

c: *Why did they feel that?*

p: They said [*West coast agent voice*]. "Roman baby, you know, Shakespeare is box-office poison."

c: *That voice sounded very familiar? Who was it?*

p: That's the voice of Hollywood.

c: *I'd know it anywhere.*

p: It would sound better with a thick cigar.

c: *People are always analyzing you because of your work.*

p: I hate that. They are free to analyze me, but I don't like to analyze myself.

c: *Does it bother you when other people say, "In this part of the movie we can see Polanski's childhood"?*

p: No, that's wonderful. Let them do it. It creates the legend, and then it's easier to get money to make the next movie.

c: *But your own childhood has such dramatic things in it. I don't think that anyone who hasn't lived through Europe during the war can have any idea what it was like. You've been very close to death twice as a kid. I'm thinking of the one incident when you were on the hillside picking berries.*

p: I was close to death many times, but there's no point of lamenting about my childhood. Think of any child in India, Pakistan, and Vietnam. We just don't have contact with these people. I was living in the countryside since I escaped from the ghetto, just before the liquidation.

c: *This was Warsaw?*

p: No, this was Krakow. It wasn't as terrible as in Warsaw. In Warsaw people were virtually dying in the ghetto. The Krakow ghetto was liqui-dated before they started dying of starvation and they were sent to the concentration camps. My mother was taken first, and about a month later I escaped because we knew they were going to liquidate and my father cut the wires. It was quite easy to get out of the ghetto, it was no problem. The problem was to survive outside. He cut the wires about seven or eight o'clock in the morning—I don't remember, it was very early. We could see Germans coming because they used soldiers for liquidation to send people to the concentration camp, and that was the last time I saw him. First I stayed with some friends of my father, and subsequently family friends, and eventually with people I didn't know. Then I ended up in the country. It was my first contact with the country. I was seven and a half and I lived there for a few years. It was a very backward group of people but they were quite good to me. They were not like the people in [Jerzy Kosinski's novel] *The Painted Bird* which if you didn't read I suggest you do because it's a very similar childhood.

Once I was there picking berries and I saw some German soldiers on a horse cart, and I just ignored them. Then I heard the whistle of a bullet. It was the first time I heard such a thing, and then I heard the clap of the explosion. I looked in the direction and saw they were just shooting at nothing to do with me. They just let out a shot.

C: *Just for fun.*

P: I don't know why you and Kenneth Tynan picked that story because I went through much more drastic situations. I was bombed and people tried to kill me, I was in so many things like that. Being shot at is just an innocent thing. I don't know how many things like that have happened to you. Maybe there was a flower pot that fell behind you that you didn't hear because there was a bus passing at the same time, and you didn't hear the noise. To me, a much more dramatic incident was when I was in the ghetto just before the liquidation and I saw a group of old women being led somewhere by German soldiers. One was very old and could hardly walk and was sort of staggering behind. I was on the other side of the street. This German officer was pushing her and shouting at her in German, and suddenly he drew a gun and shot her in her back. The blood exploded. It was all so fast. This woman fell down and I ran into a doorway and hid myself under the stairs and stayed there for maybe an hour. That was a really shocking and terrible experience in my life, not the one when they were shooting at me. For the first time in my life—I was maybe seven, I don't remember exactly—it scared me so much that I couldn't forget it for years afterward. It's much more frightening when you see something than when it happens to you.

C: *Who was there to explain that sort of thing? Did you assume that's the way the world was, that people shot people constantly, that people tried to kill people all the time? Or did you know you were going through a particularly bad part of the world?*

P: Well you see, the child accepts everything. That's just reality. You can put a child in a white room and it will accept this as reality. Throughout the war I ate boiled flowers, sometimes with milk, for three years, and I thought that was the normal food. Sometimes there was sugar or something. And I wasn't particularly unhappy about this. I know now that people kill and start wars because they like it. We have to accept that it's part of human nature. It's evolutionary. We are built this way. The other part of human nature—the civilized mind—rebels against this. But there wouldn't be wars if people didn't want wars. People enjoy killing and fighting.

C: *But did you know that there was somebody your age—me—growing up somewhere else in the world in a completely peaceful place?*

P: Of course. I'll tell you another episode which will explain exactly how I felt. About two or three years later I was living in the country and I was picking berries again. It was all we could do—pick berries or mushrooms and help with the harvest—because they had only an acre and a half for the whole family. There was hardly anything to eat. Anyway, I was picking berries on the hill. It was toward the end of the war, summer 1944. Very hot. Summer in Poland is very hot, winter is very cold—like in Canada. I was in a little birch wood, and all you could hear was the summer noise of the insects. Suddenly I heard a different noise. I couldn't understand what it was, and I thought it was an airplane. I looked up and saw hundreds of American planes going east. And then a new noise, and I could see the explosions of the German artillery. This was one of the most beautiful moments of my life. It was bringing such hope and expectations for something to come. And I was just hoping that none of the planes would explode. They did occasionally and I would see the white parachute, and then I was hoping he would come over this way and I would be able to talk with him. It was a moving experience. It was beautiful. This noise is very important for me, and I used it in one film. As a matter of fact I used it in *Macbeth*, but no-one would notice.

[*Cavett moves from his interview chair for a commercial break during which he introduces and advertises various products.*]

P: I didn't know you did these things. When I was on your show before you didn't do this.

C: *I'm in the big time now.*
P: You do the same thing I'm doing now.

C: *What's that? Selling?*
P: It's sort of a tap dance that one asks you to do in order to work again.

C: *A tap dance? Is that what you feel you're doing because your movie's appearing and you're being taken around town and propped up?*
P: That's the way I feel. I would rather talk to you in a café.

C: *Let's go! Let's take everybody with us! I said to you during the break that somebody who's been through a nightmarish childhood must feel a certain contempt for people who haven't been through it because they've had it so much easier. Maybe you don't?*
P: No, I don't have any contempt. Sometimes I feel anger when they come up with issues that seem to be ridiculous in view that they never went through any kind of hardship that could have made them talk differently. I want to be clear that I'm quite sure that this experience does very little to a child, strangely enough, as far as your creative life is concerned. Maybe it can mold your life and character and personality, but for the creative life, the lessons are much more important. I can see that the people who went through the war between eighteen and thirty, I would say, were tremendously marked. Any of my colleagues of the generation that is a little bit older can't talk about anything else but the war in their films and literature.

C: *But a child absorbs it.*
P: A child absorbs it as reality. He didn't know better before.

C: *Maybe you pity yourself more when you're older? I can't really talk on the subject because I've never been through anything quite like it. You said*

you've faced death several times. Does that give you a kind of feeling—and
I'm trying not to make some fatuous comment—that every day you've gotten
since then is a bonus?

P: It took me a very long time to come to this conclusion. Strangely
enough, I came to this conclusion only two years ago, that every day is
a bonus. I didn't have this before. I was very cheerful and optimistic,
and I still am. But my personality has changed a little bit. When I was
sixteen I was being murdered, literally, by a thug. [*Shows Cavett the scars
on his head.*]

C: *I've read about these scars.*

P: Later on in the hospital my father and everybody was lamenting
about how stupid I am and about how I could have been killed. I could
not believe it. When you escape close death, you don't believe it.

C: *As I understand that story, a guy was going to sell you a bicycle and said
to meet you in a certain place?*

P: I was sixteen and I was racing bicycles. A very popular sport in
Europe. That was my future—I really wanted to be a racing champion.
It was very difficult to get racing gear and he offered to sell me a bicycle
for a very cheap price that from his description sounded like a marvelous racing bicycle. We had this appointment in this old German
bunker. We walked down there, I had the money in my pocket. He was
holding a torch made out of newspaper. It was raining outside. My
friend was waiting on the other side of the double carriageway where
the street was, in a doorway. I don't remember exactly how it happened. We were talking about the dirt on the floor and how people are
terrible—these were his last comments. I was looking for this bicycle, I
could hardly see the end of this long bunker. He said it was around the
corner, and I said, "There is no corner." Then he struck me. It was so
unexpected for me. In the brief short moment before I lost conscious-
ness—I know I lost it so quickly because I felt only one blow, and I have
five scars—I thought I had touched a live cable and was electrocuted.
Then I thought, "No, somebody hit me." I could not believe that it was
this guy whom I had met a couple of weeks ago and had walked around
with a little bit. I treated him as a friend, he was a very young man.
Only when I saw him above me asking for the money, I understood it

was him. He took my money and my watch and ran away. I got out through an escape window, and there was my friend.

C: *The guy had left you for dead?*
P: No, no, no. My head happens to be very hard, and probably it was the moment when I became either an idiot or a genius. Something has happened since then that my career went straight up in a line to the Dick Cavett show.

C: *You may even go higher. Who knows?*
P: You never know, indeed.

C: *Didn't the man turn out to be a murderer that they wanted?*
P: They caught him. I said to my friend, "Run after him." There was a rubbish truck that was passing. They grabbed him and pulled him in, and he happened to be a murderer. He had killed three people before.

C: *You never used those actual incidents in a film?*
P: Actually the very first film I did when I was in film school—which was never finished because the lab screwed up the negative—was about this incident.

C: *There are so many things I would love to talk to you about.*
P: Don't be shy.

C: *Do you hate certain members of the press for the way they treated you after your wife's murder?*
P: Well, yes. To be honest, I do. But I wouldn't call it hatred now. It's somehow evolved into indifference. I simply don't read it. I try to avoid it.

C: *I don't know what you think people deserve to know or how much business people have knowing about what's called "The Sharon Tate Case"—though there were other victims. Is there anything good that has been written about it?*
P: Well, I just don't read, for my own good. It would be silly of me to say that absolutely everything written by the press is obnoxious. This is impossible. I'm philosophically orientated and I know that there are always mutants. It's the principle of life and evolution. But in general

I despise the press tremendously for inaccuracy, for its irresponsibility, for its often even deliberate cruelty. And all this for lucrative purposes.

C: *Every time the subject comes up there are people who claim they know something that never came out in the papers. The way people descend on an event like this is sort of strange.*

P: Well, this is part of human nature. I was accused of being one of the accomplices. It was like a great psychological test. Everybody saw it from his angle, his point of view, and was looking for the culprits in the area which would be somehow related to the way he was thinking. You know what I mean? I don't want to be more specific about it.

C: *I think I do. Did it seem that you could never go into public again?*

P: Yes, it lasted for a very long time. It lasted for a good eight months, I would think. And then when I started working again, I didn't want to do anything like this show for example, or any interviews. Somehow under the pressure of the people who gave the money for the film and took a great risk, because it cost several million dollars—three million dollars, let's be specific—for their sake I thought I have to do it. And I'm doing these things. But I would feel better if I did not have to talk and feel part of the public life. I was desiring it when I was young, when I was in film school and later.

C: *The celebrity part of it?*

P: Yes. I wanted it. I wanted it very much. It was part of this history of cinema, part of Hollywood.

C: *I wondered if at the time you just felt, "I can never go back to work."*

P: You see, right after that everybody was saying, "Go back to work." At the time I was in the middle of a film. Not shooting, but in the middle of preparation of a film called *The Day of the Dolphin.* Everybody said, "Work, work. That's the best medicine." I remember talking to Stanley Kubrick on the telephone. He was the only person who said, "I'm sure everybody tells you go to work." "That's right." "I know you can't work. Why don't you just go away, do some sports or something. And there will be a moment when you feel like getting out of the room." Incredible—I remember that. You know, he's very interested in everything—like I am, by the way. We'd spend endless hours talking. I could see he was trying to understand my feelings and I don't blame him for it. It's part of being a film director. He's a very wise man.

C: *I thought you gave a very good answer when people ask you how on earth could you do bloody drama like* Macbeth *after what you went through. But you pointed out that anything you did they would have said was absurd. If you'd done a comedy, they would have said, "How could he do a comedy after that?"*
P: Precisely. Everything is related to your life. That's how people see it. People see this film more bloody than it really is. I mean, it's much less violent than the average so-called violent film. Much less. It's as much as we can expect from *Macbeth*. That's about all.

[*Henry Morgan joins as Cavett's next guest*]

M: *Let me ask Roman a question. I was fascinated while you talked. You said you discovered—or that you believed—that people like to kill. Then you said you saw the American planes coming overhead and you felt so marvelous or relieved, or whatever. Do you think the Americans in the planes liked to kill?*
P: I think that war exists because it's part of human nature. Looking at it from the evolutionary angle, I think that when men had no more serious enemy in the animal world, the only enemy was another human being. That's the way it worked. Our history for the past two million years was killing. That was the men's sport. I think, incidentally, that if you got rid of all males, there would be no wars.

C: *Why do you say that at a moment when Golda Meir and Mrs. Indira Gandhi are quite warlike?*
P: You can talk only about averages. You can't take one woman as an example. You can talk about male and female personality only if you talk about averages.

M: *You saw the American planes coming by overhead and you felt a thrill. You knew they were killers. Are there good killers and bad killers?*
P: At that time, I didn't have the necessary knowledge to be able to philosophize this way. To me they were the saviors.

M: *I just wondered, because I think you're quite right. So many people have this overpowering aggressiveness and they have to get rid of it somewhere.*

P: Imagine you are a Martian observer just sent here, in a kind a space ship from which you can watch this civilization. You'd think that war was inherent, that this is a very primitive species. And when you look at history, hardly any war makes sense. In the Renaissance you could talk about just wars and unjust war. Now you can't even talk about it in these terms. The only thing you can do is to end up with knowledge, ethical knowledge, with ideologies and vitalism, with religions.

M: *They've tried all that for two or three thousand years.*

P: No, they didn't try that, I'm sorry. Objective science and knowledge has existed only for three centuries. Before that, all knowledge and philosophy was subjective. It's only when you start doing it abstractly, with mathematics, that you can have certain knowledge about the world, when you are not emotionally involved.

M: *But you can't mathematicalize human emotions.*

P: Certainly you can. Why not?

M: *Well then you're going to live in a police state you've never even heard of.*

P: But that's what you do. You math . . . how did you say?

M: *Math . . mathe . . . I wouldn't say it again. This is what I really meant. [Indicates Cavett.] Look at him. Now here is an intellectual. I don't mean it pejoratively. A bright, aware, quiet, peaceful man. Do you think he could become a killer?*

P: But you cannot talk about one person. I wonder how would he act if he had five hundred people around him involved in some kind of uprising. He would run with them. He would maybe step on someone. It's entirely different.

I think that the only problem is the population explosion, because man did not kill so much of his own species when other species were his enemies in this early evolutionary era. He killed just to eat. But at one stage other men became his enemy and he began to kill his own species. Other species have very strong inhibitions about killing themselves.

Even rats don't kill themselves. But when you put them into a confined area, then they start eating themselves and fighting each other.

C: *Speaking of violence, how do they decide what rating a movie like yours gets?*
P: In the United States, first it had an 'X' rating. Nobody would touch it. The major company that distributes the film—Columbia in my case—would not release it with an 'X' certificate, so I was forced to discuss and argue with the ratings board. Eventually they said if I do some cuts in the film, they will give it an 'R' certificate. Strangely enough, in England it had an 'AA' certificate without any problem, which means that anybody older than fourteen can go unaccompanied. I must say that when I was showing this film to the board, some nine or ten people, and I discussed it with them, I could feel a strange prejudice. They were looking at this film not as a film made by a director. They were looking at it through the filter of my particular predicament. Somehow I could feel they felt uneasy, and things which otherwise would not seem violent looked a bit indecent to them.

I know they were prejudiced because a friend of mind flew on a plane with the head of the ratings board. Apparently a long time before I even finished the film he said to my friend, "You know how many gallons of pig's blood they used?" And he said the number—seven or eight or twenty. Which of course is an idiocy because we never used pig's blood. We used a mixture of Nescafé and food coloring and milk and glycerine. That's my invention—it looks better than stock blood which looks like ketchup. And no-one will ever know how much of it was used because you do as much as you need for a particular scene. You just make it in the morning. But the fact that he mentioned something like that shows that he was watching for me, waiting for me around the corner.

C: *Do you feel that wrecked the film?*
P: No, it didn't in all honesty. It even it helped the film. Maybe those two or three areas where I made cuts were a little bit too explicit. But in general, the film as I told you is not that bloody. Right after the short prologue of the three witches, the action proper starts with the line "What bloody man is that?" Any production trying to go away from this would be a necessary false one. But people are just thriving on the fact that it's me and I have this reputation, and that I've tried to make it more bloody.

Incest Is Interesting

D E R   S P I E G E L / 1 9 7 4

S: *When* Chinatown *was released in America and England, everyone said it was your comeback film.*
P: Absolute nonsense. I never needed a comeback because I never lost faith in my ability as a director. They wrote garbage like that because they thought my last films *Macbeth* and *What?* were complete rubbish. I have a completely different opinion: those films are every bit as good as my others. These people don't have a clue about cinema.

S: *What does cinema mean to you?*
P: A difficult question. You could just as easily ask me what the meaning of my nose or right arm is. True cinema is a film that has specific, independent, dramatic, and visual qualities. It has to be an object that can almost be physically touched, like a sculpture perhaps. The atmosphere of a film is the most important thing. Very early on I was fascinated by the moods and atmospheres which emanate from places and people. People in certain situations—in moments of terror, for example—especially interest me. They live more intensely, and we're able to learn more about who they really are.

S: *How did you become interested in the cinema?*
P: During the occupation they played lots of American films in Krakow and I couldn't get enough of them. As a young boy I just

From *Der Spiegel*, 16 December 1974. Reprinted by permission. Translated by Joshua Kronen and Paul Cronin.

flipped out seeing all this stuff. When they finally sealed the ghetto we couldn't go to the cinema any more, but the Nazis screened weekly propaganda newsreels on the wall in the market place. I found a place through the barbed wire where I could see them. As soon as I managed to get out of the ghetto I began selling newspapers to earn enough money so I could go to the cinema. By then [the German film production company] UFA films were playing in the theaters and the Nazis wanted the Poles to see them, but the Poles thought it would be unpatriotic. I remember graffiti like "Only pigs go to the cinema" on the walls, but it didn't matter to me at all. Hell, I just wanted to see films—I was completely obsessed.

s: *Where did the idea for* Chinatown *come from?*
p: I'd always wanted to make a detective film. Just like everyone who loves cinema, I adore Hollywood detective films and Chandler and Hammett's books, which are better than the movies adapted from them. But I hesitated for a long time before returning to Hollywood because basically I wasn't prepared for it, because—well, you know what happened there. But then I realized I absolutely wanted to make *Chinatown* and I just got over myself.

s: *Was it difficult for you?*
p: Yes, not so much because of Hollywood but because it became clear to me rather quickly that *Chinatown* would not be so easy to direct. I was fascinated with certain ideas and realized I had to limit my imagination.

s: *How did you come up with the title* Chinatown? *Was it because the denouement of the film takes place there?*
p: No. From the very beginning the film was called *Chinatown*, even when we didn't know the final scene would be set there. The title simply represents the film's mysterious atmosphere. Jack Nicholson's detective character had experienced something important and disturbing—the violent death of a woman. Now he meets a new woman, Evelyn, who has something threatening and impenetrable about her, something that's somehow Chinese in nature. Chinatown represents this woman who Nicholson doesn't really understand.

In addition to the detective story and the idea of societal corruption, the film is also very much a mystery about a man and woman.

s: *But the final scene does take place in Chinatown.*
P: We had several ideas for the final scene but I didn't like any of them, though it was clear to me that the woman would be accidentally shot by the police. I wrote the ending we used right before we filmed it. I just had the feeling that the finale had to take place in Chinatown—a real setting—in order to lead all the allusions to some kind of conclusion, otherwise the whole thing would have been intellectual and contrived game playing. Chinatown, whether it refers to the place or the woman, represents Nicholson's fate, something he keeps having to face up to.

s: *Is it true you argued with the author of the screenplay over the ending?*
P: Yes. He wanted the bad guy, old Noah Cross, to die at the end, after being shot by Faye Dunaway, at all costs. I felt this was too romantic, too much of a happy ending. I wanted the film to end in utter tragedy, with the Faye Dunaway character dying for no reason at all, and for her father—with whom she'd fought over for the child they have together—to get away clean, just like most bad guys really do.

s: *It seems you often have a specific kind of woman in mind for your films.*
P: I couldn't say for sure. Perhaps women who are outside of the norm—who have an unusual, somewhat neurotic character—are the kinds of people who instinctively interest me when I'm making my films.

s: *In* Chinatown, *the detective discovers a political scandal: the water reservoir in Los Angeles is being secretly tapped. He also discovers that the heroine had an incestuous relationship with her father, who is behind the whole water affair. Which is more important for you in the film, the water scandal or the incest?*
P: The incest, which is the real cause of the catastrophe in the end. In reality, the capitalist swindle with the water and land of Los Angeles doesn't bother anyone. But the incest—this private scandal—is really exciting and I'm a bit disappointed it doesn't come through more

persuasively. The film would have been more sensational if I could have emphasized the affair more, and it certainly would have got more publicity. But unfortunately the plot made that impossible.

s: *Although* Chinatown *is a Hollywood production, it often comes across as being very un-American.*
p: Fortunately, yes. I wanted to make a Polanski film. Hollywood takes its heroes far too seriously by depicting them one-dimensionally and untarnished, something that bores me. It's much more exciting to have differentiated and torn figures, like in *Chinatown* where the characters are full of deep human weaknesses but still remain sympathetic. The comic side to the story was also important to me, so occasionally I made the hero a little laughable, like when he complains about his lost shoe. I would have liked to include more of these kinds of little details in the film.

s: *Is the film also a commentary on the United States?*
p: I didn't set out to say anything in particular about America, but the film does mirror something of the condition of the United States with all its intrigues and scandals, though you find these things in any country where money and power matter. A film that doesn't make any statement at all about society—and ourselves—would be completely empty. If *Chinatown* didn't have certain moral and critical qualities under the surface, I wouldn't have made the film. It's also about the difficulty of learning the truth, whether about politics or the relationship between a man and a woman.

s: *In Hollywood there is an increasing tendency towards violence. Your film seems very conservative in comparison.*
p: The violence you usually see in movies bores me. It seems so infantile and dumb because it's so inhuman. If you show someone on screen who is either the victim of violence or the perpetrator, you have to make it clear that they're a specific person and not just an object in a game, that something living, delicate, and loved is either injured or destroyed. I hope this notion come through in *Chinatown.*

s: *Does violence fascinate you?*

p: No. It interests me. It has to interest me—as a serious human expression, as a mysterious but somehow unavoidable fact. It's not just a sensation for me, rather something very basic. When I was eight years old I was attacked and robbed in Krakow. Someone nearly bashed my skull in with a stone wrapped in newspaper. He hit me five times, very hard. When I woke up, I saw the blood running over my face and eyes. And ever since that day, whenever I'm standing under the shower, I feel the blood running over me.

Showing the Work as Accurately as Possible

CHARLOTTE KERR/1976

K: *You have been rehearsing* Rigoletto *at the Bavarian State Opera since the beginning of September. You are also a perfectionist. Is it possible to combine repertory theater and artistic perfection?*
P: Only for a single show!

K: *You mean just for the première or for a single opera production?*
P: Both. Theater isn't a factory—we're not working on an assembly line where people forget about the meaning of their work and why they're here. This just isn't possible in the theater. The thing is that trade union bosses, who've never had access to an artistic way of life, have a different work ethic. It would be wrong to demand regular overtime from the choir, the soloists, and the orchestra. But as a rule it would also be wrong not to run over five or ten minutes when necessary. I think rules should be directed by common sense and interpreted fairly flexibly. But I didn't encounter these kinds of problems here.

K: *Why opera now? What has drawn you to the world of complete make-believe?*
P: Unlike film, theater is a silent agreement between actors and audiences to accept the stage as a given reality. If two actors approach each other with their arms extended in front of them because someone has said it's dark, the audience accepts this as part of the

From *Süddeutscher Zeitung*, 28 October 1976. Reprinted by permission. Translated by Moritz Gimbel and Paul Cronin.

wider consensus. What I like about opera is that it takes this to the extreme because everything is defined in the greatest detail by the text and music. Film, on the other hand, has to create everything as realistically as possible. If I say there's a forest, I have to show it.

K: *What role does music play in your life? Do you have formal musical training?*
P: I love music but I'm a total dilettante. Music moves me, that's all. I don't think you have to be a musical expert to stage an opera, otherwise I'd be the conductor. Quite the contrary in fact: expertise could be a disadvantage because it can hinder an intuitive and spontaneous approach.

K: *With film there are close-ups to explore a character's emotions. Do you miss the ability to do this with opera? Or does musical emphasis take the place of such things?*
P: Yes, I do miss the close-up. But music does indeed provide an emotional substitute.

K: *Why did you choose* Rigoletto?
P: First, because of the music. Second, because it has a lot of characters that interest me, much more than *Lulu*, for example. Verdi's story is full of such multidimensional characters. Take the Duke: every inch a villain, but at the same time young and capable of love. He leads us through his feelings for Gilda. And Rigoletto himself has many negative attributes. But though he's bitter and jealous, he remains the archetypal loving father of the nineteenth century. He's a victim. Every character has real depth—they aren't black and white—and this is what I've tried to work on, including the smaller roles.

K: *The scene changes, done by simply moving a single façade, are reminiscent of cross fades or cuts in a film. Did you consciously employ cinematic devices?*
P: Forget about film when you talk about opera, just as I have to forget about film when I'm directing it. The reason for the set design with all its movement is simple: this opera house has such fantastic stage technology it would be a waste not to use it. I don't know if you

noticed that all the changes are inspired by music. If I have the basic musical pattern in my head, I'm able to develop it further using my imagination. I've never actually seen *Rigoletto* performed. I just listened to recordings and looked at pictures of previous performances, so I knew what I *didn't* want. But I would always prefer to stage an opera I hadn't seen before. To do so means remaining in a state of innocence.

K: *What is it you want to show audience with your interpretation of* Rigoletto?

P: The work, as accurately as possible. Nothing has been changed. Perhaps people expect something extraordinary, crazy, and revolutionary, like the story set in a modern shopping mall or a meatpacking factory. I hate that. My aim is to find new ways to express emotions, passion and feelings.

Interview with Roman Polanski

PASCAL BONITZER AND NATHALIE HEINICH/1979

Q: *Did you have any problems with the distributors over the length of* Tess*?*
A: The distributor himself, Richard Pezet, said to me, "Roman, we don't mind how long the film is." I remember his exact words. But the producer Claude Berri was much more worried. Today I wonder if it wouldn't be more interesting to try and make another version of the film, a more "popular" one, to see how it goes down in some of the provincial towns or the inner cities. I know that the people who've sat through *Tess* with subtitles and Dolby stereo in Paris are happy with it, and no one's told me it's too long. But you never know—making another version could be an interesting experience. On the other hand, the film has done just as well in the provinces as in Paris. In fact I've just come back from the office where I saw the figures, and it's actually doing better.

Q: *Would the "popular" version be shorter?*
A: Yes, I think so. After all, most people don't have time to sit through a three-hour film. They're used to a faster pace and are frightened of spending that much time in the cinema. It's the same with literature, with books that have a description of a piece of paper that blows away and floats about the place, too light to blow away completely but too heavy to stay on the ground. It goes on for half a page. It's certainly like this in the novel *Tess of the D'Urbervilles.*

From *Cahiers du Cinéma*, December 1979. © *Cahiers du Cinéma*. Reprinted by permission. Translated by Paul Cronin and Remi Guillochon.

Q: *We felt the film needed to go on for three hours. Do you think you would be able to make a shorter version of the same story?*

A: The experiment would appeal to me but I don't think it's possible to change the pace and still make the same kind of film stylistically speaking. There are some people who tell stories slowly and there are singer-songwriters who do it in five minutes. Having said that, I'd like to try this experiment one time just to see what it's like.

Q: *Recently there have been two big films, big in every sense of the word: Coppola's* Apocalypse Now *and your own. We get the impression that films like this are just too big to be seen on television.*

A: These films take advantage of what the medium of cinema has to offer, that's all.

Q: *But many films today take the style, form, and size of the television screen into consideration. I can't imagine seeing your film on television.*

A: Television has such a limiting effect on your senses that you can only show material that's immediately arresting. This is why the news and sports broadcasts do very well because they're all about current events, and you really don't know what's going to happen next. Television is like a newspaper, but cinema is like a book. Your observation is correct though a little superficial because television isn't in competition with cinema. It's not the size difference that's important, as television resembles cinema more and more these days. The quality will improve, the sound will be stereo and someday TV screens will cover an entire wall. I'm certain of it.

Q: *What I find surprising is that in the 1950s there used to be large television sets, yet today it's the opposite.*

A: But those tiny televisions are gadgets—they're made to be carried about. I assure you that bigger and bigger televisions are being made. You're blind not to see it! People want them big. The bigger a television is, the more it invades our homes. The difference between film and television is that cinema is a group experience. The essential thing to consider is that you're surrounded by a crowd. It's what man has been looking for in entertainment since ancient times. It's what Greek theater, the Olympic Games, the Catholic church, and rock 'n roll concerts are all about. The growth of the record industry hasn't eliminated the phenomenon of the live concert performance. Quite the opposite in fact.

Q: *What we meant is that for some time we haven't had the chance to see films in Paris that hark back to the golden age of cinema, films like yours and Coppola's.*
A: I'm very flattered you say that because I'm a fan of those films. After watching *The Children of Paradise, Devil in the Flesh, Beauty and the Beast,* and *Forbidden Games,* it's very clear that these films offer audiences the kinds of things that deserve to be seen again and again.

Q: Tess *seems to confirm that cinema is still the most universal of all the arts.*
A: What's wonderful and very encouraging is that people are going to see the film, even outside the big cities, as I said. Yet many people told me it was sheer madness to make the movie. Even I had my doubts.

Q: *What were you worried about? The romantic side?*
A: No. I know that people like romance and real stories, and these are just the kinds of films I want to make. This means a lot more to me than the best reviews I could ever hope for. It's wonderful that audiences go and enjoy what cinema has to offer.

Q: *Don't you think that television has altered the way people perceive images so radically that when they see old films, it's almost as if they are rediscovering cinema.*
A: Yes, they're astounded.

Q: *Returning to the* Apocalypse Now *analogy and what you were saying about the collective experience of cinema, it's understandable that this idea works with Coppola's film because it's a war story. But* Tess *is a romance based on a classic English novel.*
A: All I'm saying is that television is the experience of being alone in front of your set. It's one thing to be by yourself and another being with a crowd—the feeling is quite different. The fact is that with

cinema there are people around who become part of the performance, while television isn't such a show. The history of mankind reflects the story of King Midas: man needs to tell stories and share them with other people. That's how cinema works, by word of mouth. A member of the audience will say to a friend, "I saw such and such a film—you ought to go see it." If you stand by the counter in a cinema you'll see that very few tickets are sold without this kind of recommendation. The most common cinema-goers are couples—people rarely go to the cinema by themselves. Being alone in an empty auditorium is nerve-racking.

Q: *It is easier to appreciate a film if there are a lot of people watching it. You can't involve yourself with a character the same way when watching television. You need to feel part of a group.*
A: This notion of group participation is bizarre. I saw *Apocalypse Now* in a room with just me and Philippe Sarde. Then I saw it again at Cannes in a packed auditorium and I can assure you it was a quite different experience. The critics who see films on their own really don't know what they're missing. Even when a film isn't good you experience it differently when you see it in a packed cinema. You might not agree with how the people around you are responding, but it's still very different.

Q: *What you're saying applies even more so with theater.*
A: Of course. Imagine an actor performing only for you in an empty theater! Even the King has his entourage. He would never watch something by himself, otherwise there would be too much intimacy.

Q: *When you see one of Coppola's films in a packed cinema in America, it's understandably impressive because of that country's involvement with the Vietnam war. The spectacle of the war creates a certain amount of solidarity amongst audiences. But what about Europe? And* Tess? *What could bring a European audience together so they see the images collectively?*
A: My dear friend, if I knew that, I'd be the richest man alive! You never know things like this until the last moment. All you can do is keep the faith.

Q: *Allow me to phrase the question differently. Could you have made* Tess *in America?*

A: Let me remind you that David Selznick owned the rights to Hardy's book for many years. He had two projects close to his heart: *Gone with the Wind* and *Tess*, which he never managed to make. The film today is very much a European work, there's no doubt about it. I'm European, I can feel it. I feel most comfortable here. The countryside, the atmosphere—it's all second nature to me.

Q: *But a version of* Tess *has already been made in America.*

A: Yes, MGM made a film in 1924 that had a happy ending. [*Reading from an encyclopedia*] "One of the most popular releases of 1924 was . . . Mr. and Mrs. Marshall Neilan's version of Thomas Hardy's formidable novel *Tess of the D'Urbervilles*, scripted by Dorothy Farnum. Neilan was one of the Hollywood top directors . . . Tess was played by Blanche Sweet, then aged twenty-eight, already a veteran of fifteen years having started at the Biograph studios with Mary Pickford and the Gish sisters. There is a scene where Tess reveals to her husband (Conrad Nagel) the shameful truth about her seduction by d'Urberville (Stuart Holmes) when she was a servant in his house. After the film was completed, [Louis B.] Mayer changed the tragic ending to the happy one, much to Hardy's annoyance." [*laughter*] Later, in the era of talkies, Selznick acquired the rights and held onto them until we bought them from his estate. I have some documents compiled in 1945 that his son gave me which include an analysis of the book, costumes, locations, and characters. A hundred pages in all. You're asking me if it could have been made in America? Yes, of course.

Q: *Let's imagine the film is being made in America today. What would the main differences be?*

A: Well, it would have to be shot in Europe because you can't find those landscapes in America. And it would have to be made in France as you can't even find countryside like that in Dorset any more. You don't see many small fields bordered by hedges. Most of the fields have been widened, the hedges cut down, the roads tarmacked. It's easier to find the right kind of architecture in England, but only Britanny or Normandy still offer the same countryside and landscape. It's hard for me to tell you exactly how it would be done. Of course, if it had been me I would have fought for it to be exactly the way you've just seen.

Q: *But how would someone in Hollywood have made the film with all those obstacles?*
A: You know, there's a whole group of new filmmakers in Hollywood who are making films quite differently, who are fighting against the artificiality of the Hollywood tradition. Look at Michael Cimino, Coppola, Stanley Kubrick.

Q: *We get the impression that there isn't an American filmmaker today, apart from Kubrick, who would be capable of making a film with the same passion.*
A: I think that people are ashamed of being passionate. People's emotions are so inhibited these days, something that's developed over the past forty years, or at least since the Second World War. It's this macho side I once had myself. Getting older has helped me understand certain things. Something that was very reassuring—it was even a moving moment for me—was something Andrzej Wajda and I spoke about a few weeks ago. He feels exactly the same way. He said to me, "The people today who are trying to make the kind of films we were doing more than twenty years ago are idiots." They think they're part of the *avant-garde* but they don't understand a thing. Some people still want to make *Un Chien Andalou*, but to make a film like that today would be totally backward-looking. Look what's happening with short films. In your profession you get to see quite a few of them, yet most are full of pseudo-intellectualism, pretension, and pseudo-poetry. Nothing could be more boring.

Q: *I reread the last interview you gave to* Cahiers *ten years ago and there's one phrase that cropped up: "It really bothers me when I get the feeling that someone's trying to impress me." This is precisely what short films are trying to do: they are a quarter of an hour or twenty minutes long, and directors have one idea with which to make an impression. Unfortunately it's not only short films but nearly every film out there. Filmmakers get so harangued from every angle that they use the little freedom they have to impress the public.*

But with Tess *we were surprised to see a film that really takes all the time it needs to tell the story, and does so without looking to impress anyone.*

A: It's more a question of honesty. You need balls of steel to have honesty as a filmmaker today, because you're running an enormous risk, one that you also make others run. I think I've had a lot of opportunities throughout my life to settle my nerves, so today I feel capable of taking certain risks without being too frightened.

Q: *It also seems as if many French filmmakers don't believe in the power of cinema, but with* Tess *we get the opposite feeling. Where do you think this feeling of powerlessness come from?*

A: You shouldn't tar every French filmmaker with the same brush. You're right in thinking that amongst this group some of them could have made a film as good as *Tess,* or even better. But the whole world of art is caught in a dead end which is very hard to escape from. It's not enough for a filmmaker to be courageous. He also needs a courageous investor and producer.

Q: *In terms of how the production deal was struck, it seems that* Tess *has a very American quality. It's not for nothing that you recently returned from the United States where you learned to gamble with the vast sums producers gave you, something that hardly ever happens in France.*

A: And yet it used to happen here! Carné, Becker, and Clément were able to work in this way.

Q: *But not anymore, though there were some directors like this up until the era of the French* nouvelle vague.

A: So do you think it was the *nouvelle vague* that in some way destroyed French cinema?

Q: *Let's just say that the 1950s gave the* coup de grace *to an already declining industry, and maybe the* nouvelle vague *was one last twitch which at the time was perceived as being a new movement. Almost everyone—Truffaut, Chabrol, Demy, even Godard—tried to take French cinema forward, but it was in tatters even before they came on the scene. But let's get back to you: what kinds of things did you learn when you were living and working in America?*

A: What you learn above all is enthusiasm. This is where the spirit of enterprise that you were talking about comes from, and also from being able to admire someone else's talent and successes. There's nothing more negative than trying to ridicule other people. I learned many things in America that I'd already encountered at film school in Poland. But as I see you know the history of cinema, you're going to tell me both systems are the same thing since the Polish technique was developed by filmmakers who were in the Soviet Union during the Second World War. And Soviet cinematography was based entirely on the principles of American production which had been studied and copied in the post-revolutionary era, at a time when they had as much enthusiasm as the Americans have today. So as far as our practical studies in Poland went, I learned the American-style principles of production and direction. But ideologically speaking . . . [*laughter*]

Q: *Were most of the technicians on* Tess *English?*

A: No, most of them were French. You don't know what sort of technicians you have here! The crew on this film was the most competent and enthusiastic I've ever worked with, and everything just clicked. I should say that the executive producer Pierre Grunstein knew the technicians well enough to select only the very best and that Claude Berri was well liked among them. They were happy to work with me which meant there was a good atmosphere on set and a sense of pride. Everyone strove to do their absolute best. I've never come across such good technicians nor experienced such a congenial atmosphere over such a long period. It lasted nine months in all. The original seven-month shoot was extended because of a strike at the studio where we were working. Even the mixture of French and English technicians worked out—they got on well together. The unforgettable meals in the mobile canteen which we set up in a different place every day were a real pleasure. We worked day and night in extremely difficult conditions, yet no one was ever in a bad mood and never a bad word was spoken. When I had to make them wait hours for something they always understood why. And on top of that, we were often filming at dusk during "magic hour" which meant everything had to be done within half an hour. That's when all the madness began with everyone was running about. There was never a dull movement. It was like being in an operating theater. You'd say "Hammer!" and suddenly there were three hammers in front of you!

Q: *You had to be demanding on the crew, something which technicians appreciate.*

A: Maybe. They were all very conscious of the difficulties of the film. They worked for free for quite a few weeks, including overtime. There was a guy, the chief technician, called Dédé Thierry. He's very intelligent and set the tone for the rest of the team. He's the guy who follows the script and who you need to tell only once where you want the camera moved and it's set to the nearest millimeter! To show you how a company like SFP [Société Française de Production] works I'll give you a little anecdote. Today it's an anecdote but back then it was a real drama. Do you remember that long traveling shot on the horse in the forest? I'd found the location and we needed a certain night-light so as to be able to make it look day for night [*la nuit américane*]. Everything was ready but there weren't enough rails for the dolly—we had forty meters and needed ninety, so we called the SFP. They had some track that was a different size than ours but we asked for a hundred meters anyway and sent a little van. It left at four in the morning and returned later that night. When the technicians began to lay out the dolly tracks, they realized they'd been given only forty-five meters of track. It was a bit of a drama because we discovered this only a few hours before shooting was due to start. Dédé Thierry said to me, "Don't worry, we'll sort something out." I said, "What are you going to sort out? How will you manage it?" He joined our tracks with theirs and made a platform that rolled down onto the SFP tracks. Afterwards we understood what had happened. At SFP they'd loaded up the rails until 5 o'clock when they just stopped. If they'd been in brain surgery at 5 o'clock they would have taken off their gloves and stopped! [*laughter*] You can't make movies like that! Having said that, I should be fair: there are very good people at SFP, but they're completely swallowed up and are afraid of the mediocre attitude of the organization.

Q: *Where do you think this attitude comes from?*

A: It comes from the system. If you go to Poland you have to deal with it all day long. How can you improve the quality of an organization if the management doesn't have the right to sack useless employees? And most of them *are* useless. They arrive late without an excuse, climb up the scaffolding to go to sleep, and afterwards climb back down to discuss their next strike. The people who are interested and motivated—those who actually want to do some real work—are stifled by the others. They're scared of being branded a fascist or a scab.

Q: *The film's photography is very beautiful, without being showy. How did you move from one cinematographer to another after cameraman Geoffrey Unsworth died during production?*

A: It was very difficult for Ghislain Cloquet to take over the film from such a great cinematographer. To find yourself in the midst of a team that's used to a particular person—someone very dear to us—wasn't a very enviable situation. But Ghislain managed very well and caught on very quickly. For the first three days he looked through everything that had been shot, and to understand Geoffrey's lighting techniques he spoke with the technicians. We didn't even rearrange the shooting schedule because I felt we should just continue straight away and not stop for a minute. When we arrived on the set the day after Geoffrey's death, there was a bizarre atmosphere. It felt like there was a void, as if everyone hadn't arrived yet and an important member of the team was missing.

Q: *Tess seems to be proof that you are still able to impress Hollywood.*

A: I no longer feel the need to assert myself. Maybe that's why I'm capable of making a film like *Tess*, because I don't want to appear original or to impress anymore, or to play the *auteur*. I've always found that a little puerile, even more so today. There's nothing more assertive than success, and my desire for such things is completely natural.

Q: *Could you have ruined your career when you left America?*

A: My career was already in tatters when I got into trouble over there. I found myself in the middle of a nightmare and told myself, "It's unbelievable, all my efforts, my whole life, ending like this." But many things became clearer to me. I could understand those people who find out they have cancer and who learn to live with the idea that the end is near.

Q: *How did you overcome this?*
A: I kept my side of the bargain until the very end. I went to jail and didn't do anything for a whole year. They put a stop on two films I was working on and threw me in jail. I said to myself, "Well, it's over. I'll get out and start over again." Two days later I learned that the judge, despite his assurances, wanted to go through another trial. I said, "Enough is enough," and I left.

Q: *You could have made a small Polanski picture on your return to France, but instead you chose to make* Tess.
A: Yes, but we didn't know what we were getting ourselves into, otherwise we would never have started this. If I'd said to Claude Berri, "We're going to make a film that's going to cost twelve million dollars," he would have thought I was joking.

Q: *What was it that made you realize this wasn't a small film at all?*
A: Berri has a very romantic nature and when I introduced him to Nastassia Kinski who was passing through Paris, he fell in love with her. He said, "I've never seen a face like that. She's so moving and vulnerable. She's very much Tess." The associate producer Paul Rassam and producer Pierre Grunstein were also enthusiastic, so we just threw ourselves into it. We worked out an initial budget, then a second one and a third. Then we had all those strikes. Little by little we realized it was going to be a big project, but to begin with we were very naïve about things. It was only once we'd finished filming and looked at all the material that I really understood. I discussed it with Philippe Sarde—whose opinion I value greatly—and with Gérard Brach. We said to each other, "We have to find the right pace and style that suits the story" and decided it had to be three hours long. I told this to the distributor and he said, "Three hours? OK, it's three hours," though Claude was a little worried.

Q: *Do you think that when you tell a romantic story successfully you need a lot of time?*

A: Yes. If you pick up a book you can tell immediately whether it's a romance or a *nouveau roman* just from the weight. It's like when as a child you were happy because there was a lot left to read in a book. As you got closer to the last three pages you'd slow down to draw it out.

Q: *The more time goes by, the more difficult it is to know which country you belong to. You are Polish but you were born in Paris. You have filmed in England and America. You speak French fluently and have lived everywhere. We wonder if you don't have some sympathy for Tess, someone who doesn't seem to belong anywhere.*

A: Of course I feel a lot of sympathy for Tess, as much as anyone who's read the book or seen the film. You've forced me to think about something very interesting here, as critics always do, especially the ones from *Cahiers*. But you know, I think of myself quite simply as a film-maker. Which world do I belong to? We all know the answer to that: it's called Earth. I feel very happy on this planet. I don't know why I should especially associate myself with any particular country just because of where I was born or educated.

Q: *In a certain era people believed—maybe more than today—in national or even regional cinema, in small films that were authentically Czech or Polish. A good example is* Knife in the Water *which is thought of as a Polish film.*

A: But it is a Polish film! After all, it was made in Poland. Your question has nothing to do with nationality or the feeling of belonging to a certain country on the author's part. If your story takes place in Poland it must be Polish. If it takes place in Transylvania, it's Transylvanian.

Q: *But these days cultural regionalism matters less and less.*

A: Everything is becoming more and more international, our whole lives included. Distances have become shorter and shorter, information is instantaneous. People used to be born and die in the same place—they never traveled further than ten miles from their village. But today they take vacations with Club Med in the Pacific.

Q: *Does it mean anything to speak of European cinema?*

A: I think there is a European cinema, but the differences between European and American cinema are becoming blurred, something that's affecting all regional cultures. It's a shame because I'm for keeping as many cultures alive as possible, all these different languages and regional attitudes. Yet it doesn't change the fact that this can't go on because it runs up against the second law of thermodynamics: in a closed space like the universe things inevitably and irreversibly deteriorate. It's entropy. If you put some ink in a bottle of water it'll dissolve. There really is no morality in physics. The more communication there is, the greater the unfortunate tendency diverse languages have of leveling off towards one international language.

Q: *Why is that unfortunate?*

A: Diversity is wonderful. It's what gives life real value.

Q: *The romanticist idea is that of a character not being the source of his desires, but rather that such desires are thrust upon him from outside. In* Tess *this outside force is the name to which Tess is entitled but which she doesn't use: Durbeyfield-d'Urberville.*

A: That's what's called destiny, like a meeting on a country road that could have been avoided if her father had slipped on a banana skin.

Q: *Tess isn't full of romantic naiveté. She is overtaken by the events going on around her.*

A: She's part of a system, and going against it is just not something she would ever consider doing. With her there's no rebellion. *Tess* is also the story of a society that's impervious to anything foreign, to anything that doesn't belong or that's even slightly different. Even today an individual who tries to enter society through the fringes will be crushed.

Q: *We also thought of George Cukor's* Sylvia Scarlett, *a film that features a character who wants to change her social class and even her sex. Isn't this something that usually happens to female characters?*

A: I always get a lot more satisfaction from working with women. There are no emotional implications here—I'm talking on a purely professional level. Women are a lot more motivated, and when they play a character they give it their all. But today there are very few women who would make me want to buy a cinema ticket. There are some male stars—Marlon Brando for example—whom I would always go and watch, but not after *Superman* and *Apocalypse Now*.

Q: *Why do you think there aren't any more female stars that people want to see? In America today the big stars are usually men.*
A: I suspect it's because they've all taken their clothes off. I know that the feelings I had from seeing Vivien Leigh or Jean Simmons or Rita Hayworth have disappeared. I think Kinski will help audiences rediscover these sensations because she has a real honesty. She has no wish to show off. She's serious. With her it's real sincerity.

Interview with Roman Polanski

MAX TESSIER/1979

T: *My first impression is that with* Tess, *your personality as a director has become invisible. The story is not told as subjectively as some of your previous films, in particular* The Tenant. *Do you think that some auteurs are moving towards populist cinema while still maintaining strong personal influences over their work?*

P: It's not so much that I'm not as involved in the film, more that the narrator of the story isn't participating as directly in the action. But this has nothing to do with me—it's simply a question of narration. Take *Chinatown* for example, the story of Jake Gittes, a private detective, a film that needed an essentially subjective narrative style. I wanted to give the impression that this was a tale being told by Gittes and that everything is seen through his eyes. The audience is the invisible witness standing right behind him as the camera follows and shows us those things he can—and cannot—see.

Tess tells its story in a different way, as the audience doesn't see things through Tess's eyes. We observe, but like the narrator the audience is set apart from the characters, and there are sequences in the film where Tess doesn't belong and isn't present. The subject of the film is very different to that of *Chinatown*. It's the novel that actually suggests this different approach, and I felt it would have been quite silly to use a more subjective method when telling the story. In my opinion a story should be told by only one character, but if for structural reasons

From *Ecran*, 15 January 1979. Reprinted by permission of Max Tessier. Translated by Paul Cronin and Remi Guillochon.

it's necessary to include sequences where the leading character isn't present, you shouldn't be so subjective. You'd end up with one event seen by Tess, another seen by Angel and another by her father—though not one by Alec as he's never without Tess.

As for *auteur* cinema, I can't stand the kind of cinema that screams "Me!" It's pretentious and egocentric. What's more, if you look at most American films—unlike in Europe—the directors, Coppola, Lucas, Spielberg, and others, no longer put themselves directly into their films. They take real care and question a great deal, but there's no feeling of exaggerated subjectivity.

T: *From the start* Tess *is faithful to Thomas Hardy's novel. But even so, you've left out some important sequences, like the short epilogue where we learn that Tess has been sentenced to death. The film ends with the Stonehenge sequence.*
P: I think it's a superfluous epilogue that Thomas Hardy probably added later. At the time he wrote it, books were often serialized or published in separate chapters, and I always felt the epilogue didn't fit with the rest of the story. But I don't have any reverence or religious respect for the novel in its entirety. I'm just very keen on it, maybe because [my wife] Sharon was the one who first gave it to me. Anyway, unless we wanted an eight-hour film, we had to cut the novel down.

T: *How long was the shoot? Did you originally plan such a long film?*
P: No, originally I wanted to make the film about two hours and fifteen minutes, but I realized that to maintain the necessary rhythm we couldn't cut too much out. It's impossible to explain exactly how we filmed the script. The first screening of all the footage took weeks! There was maybe forty hours to look through. We watched and discussed it all, taking notes.

T: *Aside from the fact that you first read the book because Sharon Tate—to whom the film is dedicated—gave you a copy, what element of the story was it that most interested you? Was it Tess's unforeseeable tragic destiny?*
P: Above all the emotion. I'm an emotional person and have always been strongly connected to Polish romanticism. But of course other aspects of the book interested me too, like the irony of the father's

fateful meeting with the priest at the beginning of the story, something that transforms this girl's simple life into a tragedy. I've always been fascinated by the idea that our destinies are the result of apparently meaningless coincidences.

Tess's rebellion is often seen as something that occurs only at the end of the novel, but it's actually present all the way through. Everyone has a place within society, and rebelling against it brings grave consequences. When Tess does rebel, it kills her. Hers is an unspoken rebellion because she never really believes she can alter her position in society. This belief can be found in every society, not just Victorian England. We're not really aware of our moral contracts and the obligations that surround us, and maybe it'll be another century before we're able to question these things. Today we have a frame of reference spanning a hundred years to fully understand Tess's actions.

T: *The character of Angel Clare is something of a Marxist, but also a hopeless idealist. He is shocked when he learns of Tess's true background yet sticks to his principles. Are you being critical of idealism?*
P: I definitely liked that aspect of the book and tried to bring these ideas into the film. In fact, the episode of Tess finding the Marx book next to Angel's bed wasn't in the novel, though he does order a book from the village bookshop which upsets the father. Though we're never told what book it is I interpreted it as being Marx, as the period made this feasible. Actually, if Angel is an idealist he's just as unattractive in his own way as Alec. I even find, to a certain extent, that Alec is more honest in his cynicism.

T: *You have done a tremendous job in capturing the atmosphere of Victorian England. Do you mind being called a perfectionist?*
P: I really don't know the meaning of the word—I ought to look it up in the dictionary. The reconstruction was meticulous, needless to say, but I was equally careful in my work on *The Tenant*, though for that film it was much easier. Back then I had to build a 1960s-style Parisian apartment block, easier than both Victorian England and 1930s Los Angeles which I recreated for *Chinatown*. In *Tess* there's nothing extraordinary other than the meticulous care everyone took in making the film and whom I encouraged in a specific direction.

T: *You built a set for the final scene at Stonehenge. Why didn't you film at the real location?*

P: We used replicas of the stones to recreate the setting in the north of France which is where we filmed the sequence. Stonehenge is nothing like it was in the nineteenth century when most of the stones had fallen over and were lying flat. Now it's a tourist attraction that's gradually wearing away. It's surrounded by barbed wire and there's even a caretaker's house sitting there.

T: *How did Ghislain Cloquet cope with taking over from Geoffrey Unsworth, and at what stage did he do so?*

P: He went through all the rushes that had been shot, which amounted to maybe half the film. The last sequence that Unsworth had shot was the barn dance, one of the most beautiful scenes in the film. Of course Ghislain encountered certain difficulties, as anyone would have done who suddenly arrives on a set where the crew has bonded through their collaborative efforts, and where he is replacing a great cameraman like Geoffrey Unsworth. It wasn't easy, but Cloquet was brave enough to accept the challenge. As soon as he worked out how Geoffrey had been filming things—after discussing it with me and the crew, most importantly the head technician—it took him only a few days to understand what we needed. I personally find the visual elements of a film very important, but it should always add to the story and not burden it. I can't stand it when a film turns into a series of postcards or slides, however pretty they are.

T: *It's the first time Dolby stereo has been used in a French production. What's so good about this system?*

P: It gives a four-way stereo sound while using regular cinema projectors, and it's also a hi-fi sound reproduction. I use it only to be more expressive, that's all. I think it's important to avoid certain pitfalls, like overemphasizing one particular element, as you can end up with a film full of landscapes or a documentary on rural life in the nineteenth century. By leaving out things like this, the story becomes more realistic and moving. Above all it's about knowing how to tell a story and how to touch the audience. This is what pictorial and literary art means to me. It has to be affecting.

T: *Nastassia Kinski reminded me of Ingrid Bergman when she was working with Hitchcock and George Cukor on* Gaslight. *Did you make this connection?*

P: Not at all! It's true that sometimes there is some facial resemblance—maybe the profile—but I find Nastassia more beautiful and sensuous than Ingrid Bergman. I don't mind you making a comparison, though it might bother Nastassia!

T: *How did Claude Berri come to produce the film? It must have been quite a challenge.*

P: We'd been thinking of making a film together for some time, either this one or the pirate story, and in the end *Tess* won out. Being a filmmaker himself, Berri is more ambitious than most producers who are often failed filmmakers.

T: *You are still making genre films, even though they are virtually dead in Hollywood. What about the pirate film you temporarily abandoned. Are you ever going to do it?*

P: I'd like to. We have an excellent script, maybe the best Gérard Brach and I have ever written, but it's going to be very expensive, a lot more than *Tess*, and we're having budget problems. If we'd have known how much *Tess* was going to cost we wouldn't have made it. But once the wine bottle is open, you have to drink it. Ultimately I'm very happy with how *Tess* has turned out. The public and—for once—the critics seem to have understood the value of our effort.

T: Tess *is more English than French. What does your English period of filmmaking—*Repulsion *and* Cul-de-sac—*mean to you today?*

P: It's already been fifteen years. I don't regret these films in the slightest. On the contrary, I'm not ashamed of my work in the cinema, and in other areas too. I feel a bit nostalgic for those times. My arrival in London heralded one of the happiest times of my life. The time from then until *The Fearless Vampire Killers* was wonderful.

T: *What about Poland? Would you like to return there one day to make a film?*

P: Yes, I'm very keen to go back but it won't be easy. Things aren't going very well at the moment in Poland and I sense a cynicism in the air that I detest.

Roman Polanski

D O M I N I Q U E   M A I L L E T / 1 9 8 1

M: *What did Hollywood mean to you before you became a director?*
P: Pretty much the same as it did for all filmmakers: it was a kind of
Mecca. I saw lots of American films, I knew who the stars were and saw
Hollywood as a place shrouded in mystery. My impression changed
a bit when I found myself in film school where the approach was more
serious and scientific, and where the films were analyzed from an artistic rather than an emotional point of view. But this didn't stop us all
wanting to make it in Hollywood.

M: *Where did you discover Hollywood cinema? In Poland or in France?*
P: Every generation of filmmakers has its own "school." The one
before mine based itself on the prewar Soviet films. It was quite an
interesting period, one that preceded the arrival of Andrei Zhdanov
into the political culture of the Soviet Union with its terrible social realism. The first wave in Poland was the one with Andrzej Wadja, and for
the intermediary generation there was Italian neorealism. But we were
most interested in American films from Hollywood. For me, *Citizen
Kane* stands as perhaps the most accomplished, beautiful, and uplifting
film of all time. It's a blueprint of how cinema should be.

M: *Did you see Hollywood as the pinnacle of a career in cinema?*
P: I imagined finding myself in Hollywood one day, but at the same
time it never represented the absolute apex to me and I never thought

From *Cinématographe*, March 1981. Reprinted by permission of Dominique Maillet.
Translated by Paul Cronin and Remi Guillochon.

of living over there. I was also very keen on French cinema and planned to move to France. America seemed too exotic for me to plan a realistic future there, while France seemed more within my grasp.

M: *When did you decide you might make things work in America?*
P: Much later, after I'd spent time in France. Gérard Brach and I began to write scripts—including *Cul-de-sac*—but no one wanted to produce our work. Then *Knife in the Water* got a good write-up in England and America, and was nominated for an Oscar which put us on the cover of *Time* magazine. At the time there was a lot of interest in European cinema, especially films from Poland. Having said that, the only concrete proposition came from a guy from Twentieth Century Fox who suggested a remake of *Knife in the Water* with two American stars. I quickly realized I was wasting my time and came back to France. That was when I fell on hard times and decided to go to London which is where I made *Repulsion, Cul-de-sac,* and *The Fearless Vampire Killers.*

From America there were some vague propositions but nothing of note until when I was on holiday in the United States and Bob Evans asked me to come to Hollywood. He knew I loved skiing and wanted to talk to me about a skiing film. While I was waiting he gave me the proofs of the novel *Rosemary's Baby.* Despite my jet-lag I skimmed through the first few pages in my hotel room and wasn't able to go to bed before finishing it. It wasn't the kind of story I would ever have written myself, but there were some fascinating cinematic elements to it. I went back to London for three months to write the script and returned to Hollywood to make my first American film.

M: *Moving from the Polish production system to Hollywood must have been quite a change.*
P: They're actually very similar—almost the same thing, in fact. In theory I would say there's less of a difference between the American and Polish systems than the French and Polish ones, because the Polish one is modeled on the Soviet production system which is itself modeled on the American one. It goes back to a time when there was a good relationship between the Soviet Union and the United States. A number

of the Soviet cinema pioneers went over to study how things were done in Hollywood. This was at about the time Eisenstein was making his film in Mexico.

M: *Nonetheless, the commercial obligations are quite different.*
P: Well, that's something else altogether. It stems as much from the financing of the films as from the organization of the industry. As we all know, in America the investors are private individuals, whereas in Poland it's the state that finances films. Directors are always constrained in one way or another, unless you work with your own money, and even then . . .

M: *How can a filmmaker's personal vision be reconciled with the commercial requirements of Hollywood?*
P: In general, a decent film has a good box-office run. There are, quite simply, people whose vision is so far removed from what the public wants that they'll never be commercially successful. When I make a film I never have any doubts that it'll please the public—I'm always full of hope and optimism. The challenge is in convincing the money-men! My vision of things is so euphoric that I don't understand why absolutely everyone doesn't simply follow me in what I love doing, though of course sometimes they don't. *Cul-de-sac*, which at the time was for me evidence of the kind of films that should be being made—a film that I consider even now a great cinematic success—was a complete flop.

M: *On what criteria do the Hollywood backers base their decisions?*
P: The Hollywood crowd—and generally the people who finance films—are not very imaginative people. They're able to base their investment decisions only on something that already exists, on something tangible. When Bob Evans suggested *Rosemary's Baby* to me, for example, it was simply because he'd seen and liked *Repulsion*. A filmmaker's career is always directed by two forces: an inner force controlled by his desires and an exterior one constrained by the possibilities presented to him.

M: *Nonetheless there is that special concept in Hollywood which not all*
filmmakers benefit from, the so-called "final cut."
P: The idea of final cut emerged when independent producers started
dominating Hollywood, and today some directors have a good enough
reputation to demand it. In the golden years there were studios where
films were shot and upon which the producers depended, but today
nearly all producers are independent, which means they pitch a project
to a studio that will consider financing it. Eventually the producer
makes it within the studio framework and the studio ends up distribut-
ing it. So the independent producers have created a climate in which
it's much easier to claim the right of final cut. It used to be only the studio who had final say over things, and today this right is thrashed out
more between the director and the producer than between the director
and the studio or the producer and the studio. I remember an editor at
MGM who butchered plenty of films.

M: *Have you been a victim of this kind of treatment yourself?*
P: Yes, with *The Fearless Vampire Killers*. The producer, a certain Martin
Ransohoff, had artistic aspirations. MGM, the distributor, decided they
weren't interested in having final cut unless they felt the film needed to
be censored. At the moment of signing the contract Ransohoff told me,
"I know the American public better than you do and I'd like to reserve
the right to change the American cut of the film." Foolishly I accepted
and signed. I didn't think he had genuinely malicious intentions as
we'd worked together before. What's more, until then no one had suggested changing anything in my films. It simply wasn't done in Europe.
      Once the film was completed I realized Ransohoff was nothing like
the person he appeared to be. At heart, he was very jealous of the artistic successes of the filmmakers with whom he worked. He hated the
film and said he was going to reedit it, so he changed the music and cut
out twenty minutes which rendered the story completely incomprehensible. Naturally it wasn't a success in the United States, and made more
money in Taiwan than America and Canada put together.

M: *Do you have the impression that Hollywood has changed a lot since*
you began working there?
P: Yes. It's been a slow, gradual but probably irreversible evolution.
The advantage now is that the filmmaker is given more freedom and

benefits greatly when his film does well. The disadvantage is that the industry is suffering because the studios lie in the hands of very wealthy people like retired lawyers, certainly not real filmmakers. The studio pioneers might have been tyrannical but at least they understood the business they'd built. They also took risks. Today the new chairmen have very little to gain and a lot to loose. Their policy—above everything else—is to keep their jobs by making decisions that won't work against them. It's become the kingdom of mediocrity.

M: *And what of the future of Hollywood?*
P: That's more a question for audiences than for filmmakers. One thing is certain though: in two or three years we'll need more films. Some serious miscalculations on the part of the studios have caused production output to drop enormously, though the demand for films has actually increased, especially as cinema is an important source of material for television.

M: *When working in Hollywood, how do you reconcile your own culture with American storylines?*
P: American producers are a lot more open to all sorts of eccentricity than their European counterparts, especially the Poles. The further east you go, the more restrained it gets. It's always been America that's worked with the most unlikely subject matter. The Americans are wonderful from that point of view—they love originality. On top of that, as soon as they sense someone is talented, they don't keep him waiting around like they do in Europe.

M: *And yet a number of talented filmmakers fizzled out once they moved to Hollywood.*
P: That's because of the intellectual desert out there. The greatest talents from all fields—as much artistic as scientific or literary—have passed through Los Angeles. At the same time it's a place where there aren't any new developments—either intellectual or cultural. The city is very accommodating but intellectually speaking it's terribly impoverished. It's like an immense suburb where you rarely, if ever, see other people. There's no communication—people live as gentleman farmers, and this might explain why some people there are no longer actually creating anything.

M: *How did you manage to adapt to such a place?*

P: In general I fit in better than most of my colleagues. Milos Forman and others might feel quite cut off from home over there, but personally I never suffered in that way—not in France, England, or the United States. At the same time I never really established myself in Hollywood. Even during the rosiest period of my life when I was married and living in a house on the ocean, we went to London as soon as we had a free moment.

M: *Is the actor's mentality the same in Hollywood as elsewhere?*

P: When I arrived in Hollywood there was a surge of interest in European filmmakers. I even heard people say they wanted to make films with Wajda or Truffaut or Bergman. This came from people only slightly more informed than the general public, who generally have no idea about foreign films. There was even a sort of snobbery attached to wanting to work with us. But there have been big changes, like actors' salaries shooting up over the past five or six years, ever since Gene Hackman was paid $750,000 to replace someone in *Lucky Lady*. At the time these figures were unheard of, although today they've been surpassed. Jack Nicholson could easily get $3 million for a film, and for the last five or six years I've had the impression that actors aren't at all interested in their roles or their films, only in their salaries. It's obvious that people like Marlon Brando aren't interested in cinema anymore. Well, he's a special case. He doesn't even look at what he's doing. He gets an animal-like pleasure in outsmarting producers.

M: *How did things get so bad?*

P: Ever since independent cinema became prominent in America, quite a few producer/directors have been trying to gain more ground by negotiating with the studios over distribution within the United States. Otherwise they try to sell their films directly to distributors in different countries.

M: *Like Coppola?*

P: Yes, but to do it that way you need to have a bankable star. At the same time, these producer/directors receive such massive advances that they can allow themselves to pay unheard-of amounts to actors.

M: *Isn't the name of certain filmmakers like yourself enough?*

P: If there's a large budget then the producers want big stars as a guarantee, which is actually absurd if you look at the most recent big commercial successes. There were no stars in *Star Wars* or *Jaws* and *The Exorcist* and they still made millions of dollars. Everyone agrees it's ridiculous to pay crazy amounts of money to actors, but when you start negotiating they still ask for these outrageous salaries which end up working against their best interests. It's all going to end in catastrophe. Brando was meant to have received something like 15 percent of the box-office receipts of *Apocalypse Now*. He must have earned between eight and ten million dollars, while Coppola hasn't seen a dime yet.

M: *Hurricane is a film that you were planning to make in Hollywood.*

P: It was never a particularly worthwhile project but I needed the money and, to quote *The Godfather*, Dino De Laurentiis made me an offer I couldn't refuse. Financially it would have been very rewarding but I ended up dropping it because of my legal problems at the time— otherwise I would have done it. Having said that, we were flirting with disaster.

M: *Unlike in Europe, directors are easily replaced in Hollywood. Have you ever been faced with this situation?*

P: It doesn't happen that easily, but the investments being so much greater there means it's much more of a risk and the backers are a lot more uncompromising. If they do replace a director it's usually quite justified. With *Rosemary's Baby* I was caught up in such a situation because I had gone over budget and was behind schedule. They were telling me, "Your work is brilliant but you need to get a move on! Our New York people are putting pressure on us!" Soon after I met Otto Preminger in the studio lot and explained all this to him. He told me, "But you shouldn't give a damn! What can they do to you? They're happy with what you're doing. Yes? Well then, have you ever heard of a filmmaker getting replaced because he's gone over budget? Never." He had a point. The Americans are very professional, and believe that excellence is a guarantee of success.

Roman Polanski Wants to Quit Filmmaking

ALAIN RIOU/1982

AT THE BEGINNING OF THE YEAR, when Roman Polanski made an unexpected and sensational appearance on the French theater scene as Mozart, the hero of Peter Schaffer's play *Amadeus*—a production he also directed—many thought this was just another flight of fancy in this whimsical and ebullient *wonderboy*'s career. Now that the play has proved to be one of the rare successes of the season, there is no more talk of whimsy. Not only has Polanski completely taken to his new role—to the point of changing his whole lifestyle, which has never been so well organized—he has also calmly announced his determined decision to change profession. Is Polanski turning his back on filmmaking? The question points to a seriously felt unease, for Polanski and some of his colleagues have of late passed extremely harsh judgment on the film industry, and Polanski says he can't see himself working there again unless its "decision makers" change their ways.

"When I started out twenty years ago," he explains, "the job of the film director involved about 30 percent of dreary but unavoidable discussions with producers ignorant of artistic demands. Today the figure is 90 percent and these never-ending conversations have become so demoralizing that I just can't stand them. The film industry has fallen into the hands of profiteers who are only interested in prestige, honor, and, to put it crudely, cheap sex. I would only get involved with those people again if I found a film project that was very close to my heart."

Is it their morality you are questioning?

From *Le Matin de Paris*, 23 September 1982. Reprinted by permission of Alain Riou. Translated by Paul Cronin and Remi Guillochon.

"No, it's their compulsion to interfere, with an utter lack of decency, in areas that are completely beyond them. You have nonentities who persist in imposing their ideas on the characters, who want to change sequences, who tell you, 'This is too long' or 'This is too short' and 'Do this, not that.' So long live theater! You can still find people there who love their jobs and are really good at it. I've always been extremely fond of the stage."

Not many people know that Polanski made his first theatrical appearance as a child actor when he was only fourteen. But it was only as a director that he recently started looking for a script to produce in a Parisian theater. "Someone mentioned *Amadeus* and I was thrilled because it's a very visual piece that doesn't rely on words too much. It's very much an English play with action and real dramatic possibilities. But I certainly wasn't interested in acting in it, especially not as Mozart. The only thing we have in common is height: he was tiny. However, when I first staged the production in Poland, the director of the theater who is an old friend of mine asked me to act opposite him, and I got caught up in it. I love acting, even though it's hard work. Every evening you try to improve on the previous night's performance. An actor is at his best when he doesn't create a barrier between his own personality and the character he's playing. You become your own best friend and have to find your own balance. Right now I can't get it right every evening, but the public doesn't know that."

Though he writes his own films, Polanski doesn't plan on becoming a playwright. But he is totally absorbed in writing at the moment because he has just started on his memoirs. Not for vanity's sake, but because it's time to set the record straight. "A lot has been written about me—two books have been published recently. Not only do these hacks make up stories about me and people I've never met, but they have the cheek to invent people so they can tell stories about us together. I'm not going to sue them—it would give them too much publicity. In fact one of the writers contacted me. He said, 'If you give me an interview, the book will have a certain amount of truth. Otherwise, I'll manage without it.' As you see, I didn't have much say in the matter."

I Was Part of the Welles Group

PIOTR KAMINSKI/1983

K: *What did you think of the film school at Lodz?*

P: Making films had been my dream for a long time, but during that era of Polish Stalinism the chances of getting into such an elitist school—where the students enjoyed so many privileges—were very small. My social background didn't really work in my favor as I was neither working class nor a peasant.

K: *But you still made it.*

P: Apparently it was less important than I thought. After graduating from high school I tried to get into the theater school in Krakow as an actor but they didn't want me, and I went to Warsaw with the same result. Around this time Andrzej Wajda, who was a student at the film school, asked me to be in *A Generation*, his first full-length production. Because of this I felt a connection to Lodz—I knew the students and had worked with them, so it all seemed less inaccessible.

There was also the Young Spectators' Theater in Krakow where I acted and where Antoni Bohdziewicz, a film director and a professor at the film school, noticed me. He sometimes worked at the theater and gave me a job on a movie produced by two film students. This was in 1952. Bohdziewicz was a very fashionable and sophisticated man and a big admirer of Western culture, something frowned upon by the ruling class. Yet he had an influential position at the school as he'd been one of its original founders.

From *L'avant-scène cinéma*, December 1983. Reprinted by permission. Translated by Paul Cronin and Jerica Kraljic.

When I failed my drama school examinations it was Bohdziewicz who encouraged me to try something else, saying "Nothing ventured, nothing gained." Before sitting the exams at the Lodz film school there was a preliminary round where the professors sifted through the four hundred candidates from around the country and ruled out those who didn't stand a chance. Soon afterwards I found myself in Lodz with about a hundred other people taking the entrance exams which lasted ten days. There were screenings and different professors gave discussions about films that we'd seen, as well as acting and drawing exercises. At the end came the decisive exam before a committee. Of course the main subject was Marxist-Leninism, something I was terribly ignorant of—quite unacceptably so. But it seemed that Bohdziewicz—who must have strongly believed in my talent—had fought a battle with these committee members, these representatives of the state. He won and I got in. It goes without saying that I couldn't believe my luck. My studies there lasted five years and I graduated in 1959.

K: *Who else got in that same year?*
P: Only eight other students, among them two of my old friends from Krakow: Wieslaw Zubrzycki, a very cosmopolitan Catholic intellectual, and Janusz Majewski, an architect. Majewski eventually graduated and became a filmmaker. Wieslaw left after the second year.

The school consisted of three faculties: *mise-en-scène*, cinematography, and production. The acting department wasn't established until later. For the first year all classes were taken together, then little by little we went our own ways. The school was very well equipped, and there were actually more employees than students. We studied things directly related to the cinema, for example art direction and music, but also art history and literature. There was a complete filmmaking facility there and already in our third year we started to make films. There was a little studio outside town with electricians and mechanics, and a production office with editing and projection rooms. The most amazing thing is that even with all this there were still some students who didn't do anything. They'd got into the school by pretending they wanted to make movies, but backed out when actually confronted with all these opportunities.

K: *How was this kind of luxury possible in a country that had been so devastated by war?*

P: This is easy to explain. Lenin had said, "Amongst all the arts, cinema is the most important." Obviously in those days television didn't exist and fortunately comments like Lenin's were followed to the letter, which meant the authorities were very aware of the political importance of documentaries and fiction films. That's why we had far more freedom at the school than students of other colleges and universities, and even the whole country.

K: *Why was the school in Lodz and not Warsaw?*

P: Warsaw had been destroyed during the war and the authorities were in a hurry to establish a film school as quickly as possible. When deciding where to build production studios they opted for the city closest to Warsaw that wasn't in ruins. It was a logical choice, as Lodz is only about a hundred kilometers away. Our classes took place as much within the confines of the school as on location, which meant we really got the best practical training possible. According to the regulations, during the five years of study every student had to make two silent films, two short documentaries, a short fiction movie, and a final work, the length of which wasn't specified. But because there were so many directing students we all ended up writing and acting as much as we directed. We got through a vast amount of film stock. What was expected of us from the first year was complete familiarity with photographic techniques, so we spent weeks taking still photographs which were, on the whole, not bad, though Zubrzycki's weren't great and he was thrown out.

K: *What kinds of films did they show you?*

P: We saw lots of different things thanks to the elitist character of the school. We had access to the national archive and watched lots of films that the general public generally couldn't see. All we had to do was fill out a form and give a reason—any reason—and they would send us the film. Though some titles weren't distributed, as was always the case in the Eastern countries, copies were always kept for use by party officials and as students we were able to make use of this source ourselves. So filmmakers in Poland never really felt as isolated as, for example, writers and painters did, most of whom had to wait until 1956 and even later before discovering the fruits of a decade of Western culture. For us, Orson Welles, Kurosawa, and Buñuel were common currency. Personally, I was part of the Welles group, but there were also groups of neorealists and students who liked the heroic Soviet cinema. A friend of mine, Roman Hajnberg, admits to having seen [the Vasilyev Brothers' 1934 film] *Chapayev* twenty-five times.

K: *The atmosphere of the school during those days is legendary.*
P: And for good reason. It really was unique and totally unprecedented. The school was a true haven, a refuge of peace—both politically and culturally. Putting aside the eternal lessons of Marxist-Leninism, everything was geared toward a single goal: the efficient schooling of professional filmmakers. Those were the only criteria, even if it meant savaging the system a little bit.

Instead of going to class, students often spent time in the projection rooms. There was also a huge wooden staircase which was the epicenter of the school. It's said that postwar Polish cinema was born on this staircase, though to complete the image I should add that there was a bar at the bottom. The life of the whole school revolved around these two monuments, and whenever there wasn't a screening—which wasn't often—you could always find us there, drinking beer, talking, arguing. It just went on and on.

K: *You didn't feel the political presence of the regime?*
P: Well, of course. We had politicization lessons and even undertook military training like everybody else. This was, after all, at a time when "imperialistic forces" were preparing for the Third World War. Naturally our views on art were profoundly conditioned by the pervading ideology and we were constantly debating the virtues of "content" over the vices of "form."

K: *How did the 1956 crisis affect the school?*
P: Like everywhere else. We burned party cards and stormed the personnel offices, taking confidential files which for a few days were a great source of amusement. The office head ended up running the canteen. He fit in there perfectly—the man had found his true vocation.

K: *So today you would say that your experience at Lodz was a positive one?*
P: Yes, extremely positive, though like most of the others students I wasn't aware of it at the time. We never stopped complaining about how much time we were wasting—and those five years did seem like a very long time. But I quickly realized how much I actually owe to the school. There's no doubt it's where I learned my job.

Roman Polanski

PHILIP SHORT / 1 9 8 4

P: When I wrote at the start of my autobiography, "For as far back as I can remember, the line between fantasy and reality has been hopelessly blurred," what I meant was I simply didn't have any concept of where the limits of what's possible are. This helped me in my childhood, my youth, and even lately to achieve certain aims and goals that I wouldn't be able to reach without the conviction that everything is possible.

S: *There are people who would say that you brought your troubles on yourself.*

P: Well, I think that's total nonsense. Of course, to a certain extent you are responsible for your style of life, the life you are leading. You have a choice of the amplitude of the events that happen—the higher you get, the harder you fall. I understand there's a gentleman in England who decided to spend the rest of his life in bed. Not because he's ill, it was just his decision. Such people have very little risk of being run over by a car. So if you see it like this, then yes, I am responsible because maybe I live a fuller life than other people.

S: *You came to the West, you went to Hollywood, you married, and your wife was murdered. How did you cope when that happened? Quite suddenly out of the blue, everything that you valued was taken away.*

P: One doesn't know how one copes with things like that. At the moment one just has to make a decision: to go on living or to end it all.

The World This Weekend, BBC Radio, 22 January 1984. Reprinted by permission of BBC and Roman Polanski.

I know that in writing this book I had great difficulty in recalling those moments. I had no difficulty at all in remembering all kinds of details from my childhood, but wherever I really suffered grief—in particular this tragedy—I understand now that my mind just tends to reject certain things, to forget them completely. That probably helps me to live with it afterwards.

S: *You obviously feel you had a very raw deal from the press, both over what happened when Sharon Tate was murdered and later when the rape case was brought against you in America. Is this one of the reasons that prompted you to write your book—to set the record straight?*
P: It's the main reason, I would say. I don't think I would exaggerate if I said I was one—or maybe the person—who has suffered more abuse from the press than anybody else. If I showed you the trunks full of clippings which I keep down in my cellar you would be truly surprised. And it continues—there seems no end to it. I wrote the book to tell it as it really was from as far back as I remember. But even this seems to be a vain effort.

S: *Don't you exaggerate in your own mind to some extent? The reason I say that is you have a line in your book where you say, "Many people look on me as an evil, profligate dwarf." But I don't think many people do look on you like that.*
P: Well, I often read those sentences in the press, like "the diminutive Polish director." Whenever they talk about my physique they always take a couple of inches away, as though five foot five inches wasn't short enough. Whenever they talk about my travels they always add a few more females in my entourage. Whenever they talk about my life, they paint it in drastic and prurient colors. So no, I don't think I exaggerate. You just don't follow what's been written about me. The only person who follows it thoroughly is me.

Roman's Novel

FRANZ-OLIVIER GIESBERT/1984

G: *You've gone through hell and high-water from the Krakow ghetto to the Manson family, taking in Stalinism along the way. Are you proud of having survived it all?*
P: Not particularly.

G: *Happy?*
P: Not for the time being. But I don't rule out being so one day.

G: *If you're not proud, what made the young man inside you look back on his life in your autobiography* Roman?
P: It was time to hear it from the horse's mouth, that's all. A lot of books have been written about me where everything's been invented from start to finish. The authors didn't even bother doing any research.

G: *Can you think of any examples?*
P: It's really humiliating having to delve into these books, but there is one by a certain Kiernan, for example. Everything in it is false, from start to finish. It's complete fiction, pure and simple.

G: *The first pages of your book, which include your wanderings in Paris, feel as if they've been taken straight out of a novel.*
P: My father was not happy in France. Like all immigrants he missed his homeland, so we returned to Poland.

From *Le Nouvel Observateur*, 13 April 1984. Reprinted by permission. Translated by Paul Cronin and Remi Guillochon.

G: *Your parents then settled in Krakow. Being Jewish, they were forced to*
move into a different neighborhood after 1939. One day you saw some men
building a wall on the road and you began to cry.
P: It was the beginning of the ghetto, but I didn't spend my childhood crying. Children don't have any point of reference—they're optimistic by nature. After each round-up I was sure that things would improve
and I told myself that the Nazis would eventually realize we hadn't
done anything wrong. Pessimism, in fact, is what life experience
teaches us.

G: *Did the adults in the ghetto react the same way as you?*
P: No one ever thinks of the worst case scenario. Even people on
death row have a glimmer of hope that they'll be reprieved.

G: *What did you do in the ghetto?*
P: We went sleighing and played about.

G: *Were you frightened?*
P: Once the Nazis killed a woman right in front of me in cold blood,
just like that, and I hid under a staircase for hours. But I was more
frightened of being separated from my parents. I was eight years old
when my mother was taken away in a round-up. She never came back
from the concentration camps. Not long afterwards, on 13 March 1943,
the day the Krakow ghetto was liquidated, my father cut through the
barbed wire around the enclosure and said to me, "Get out of here!" So
I ran and ran.

G: *That's when your tribulations begin. You give us a rosy version of Jerzy*
Kosinski's novel The Painted Bird.
P: Did you want me to dramatize it?

G: *Kosinski was hunted up and down Nazi Poland, but not you. How come?*
P: I had fair hair and was able to fit in more easily than him. Kosinski
wrote a novel in which he highlighted certain things. What's more, the
book takes place on the Russian border, the most backward part of
Poland which was still pretty medieval. Today those territories are part
of the USSR.

G: *Your fate is that of Elie Wiesel or Kosinski—a survivor.*

P: I'm a toy in the hands of history, and by extension, a witness. But tragedy has never been my strong point. Nor has religion. I am, in fact, a circus performer.

G: *What got you interested in cinema?*

P: When I was in the ghetto, the Nazis sometimes showed films outside in the market-place, on the other side from where we lived, and I would watch the projection through barbed wire. It was generally Third Reich propaganda with the intermission consisting of slides which had things like "Jews = Typhoid" on them. When the Soviets arrived they inundated us with their patriotic films and I was immediately converted.

G: *What was your biggest cultural shock?*

P: The arrival of films from the West. Walt Disney and Errol Flynn quickly became my idols, and Laurence Olivier's *Hamlet* had a profound effect on me. When I left the cinema that day I was in raptures. It's a film that opened so many doors for me.

G: *Very quickly you started to make a name for yourself, and early on were involved with a children's radio program.*

P: But I didn't get into acting school because I was too up front, too different from the other candidates who were nervous and full of humility.

G: *But you were selected by the Lodz cinema school, one of the best in the world.*

P: Luckily for me, Lenin once said that cinema is the communist state's most important art form. That's how the Lodz school became a kind of safe haven for free spirits.

G: *You were then able to make your first film* Knife in the Water.

P: Ripped to shreds by the Polish official critics and then denounced by [first secretary of the Community Party] Gomulka himself! What are you driving at?

G: *That the regime gave you a chance.*

P: Do you want me to say that I owe my success to that regime?

G: *They didn't stop you.*

P: Well of course not, since I left them behind! My secret is that I lived out what my compatriots only dreamt about. Most of them were happy to live in the West only in their minds, but I was raring to escape as soon as I could, no matter what. I even imagined building a pedal-powered submarine.

G: *Do you still feel Polish?*

P: Of course, but I try to distance myself as much as possible from what's going on over there.

G: *Because there's no hope anymore?*

P: There is some. Not in Poland, but in the heart of the system, in the USSR. For starters, communism doesn't work. It doesn't take human nature into account. As a contemporary Polish proverb says, "Whether you're sleeping or standing, you'll always be paid 2000 zlotys." But that's not the most pressing concern. As we enter another industrial revolution, the Soviet system is so centralized and totalitarian that it stifles any innovation. It'll end up rotting away from inside until the empire collapses completely. Nevertheless, I think that eternal Russia will live on—along with its expansionist tradition—while my own country will steady its course towards the West. Of course, that won't stop it from being used as a doormat every now and then.

G: *After leaving Poland you spent a short time in France. Were you eager to conquer Hollywood?*

P: No, it was necessity that drove me there, not the American dream. The truth is that no one would give me any work here in France. I spent three and a half years doing nothing—walking around trying to hawk my screenplays, which were rejected everywhere. You realize that French cinema is a conservative milieu, even a little xenophobic.

G: *But isn't France a land of asylum? It's a country that has welcomed so many foreign artists.*

P: France likes her refugees only if they keep a low profile. When you're young it's very difficult to get noticed in this country, and not only as a filmmaker—I'm talking about all areas. When you're a foreigner to boot, it's even harder. The French are suspicious by nature. They'll risk their cash only on a sure thing, and it was only in England that I was able to find the backing for *Repulsion* and *Cul-de-sac*. Everything came together for me after that.

G: *And then you went to Hollywood.*
P: Hollywood is a land of leisure that you can blend into within twenty-four hours. But quite quickly I realized that the studios are run by a bunch of agents and lawyers who don't have much to do with the artistic side of things. The gulf between these people and the artists is constantly widening and their relationships can be so fraught that you wonder if some filmmakers haven't purposely tried to bankrupt their producers. Michael Cimino poured money down the drain—nearly $50 million in all—during the making of *Heaven's Gate*. It was as if he was doing it out of revenge and wanted to punish everyone. To make a film these days, 90 percent of your work consists of negotiating with those people who supply the capital. When they see you're keen on a project, they take advantage of it by increasing their demands. To make *Pirates*, my next film, I'll have accumulated ten years of bickering, rows, and frustrations.

G: *Which actor have you had the best working relationship with?*
P: Jack Nicholson is very easy to direct, even if he's a bit of a party animal. The worst lines still sound good when he delivers them. The same goes for Mia Farrow, Catherine Deneuve, and many others. Having said that, actors are in a world of their own. Most people don't generally spend their time pretending to be someone else. But if you pretend to have a limp for three months, it can be difficult to stop straight away.

G: *You've explored all cinematic genres: comedy in* The Fearless Vampire Killers, *horror in* Rosemary's Baby, *the thriller with* Chinatown *and romance in* Tess. *You give the impression of not being able to tie yourself down.*
P: I like cinema too much to be happy doing only one thing.

G: *Which film are you least happy with?*
P: *Repulsion*, where I had very limited financial resources. You can see what I mean with all the little details in the film.

G: *And your favorite film?*
P: *The Fearless Vampire Killers.* It's an amusing and unpretentious film, and I really enjoy watching it.

G: *And because it was when you met the woman of your life, Sharon Tate?*
P: Yes, the film reminds me of the happiest time of my life. It's Proust's madeleine to the power of a thousand. All my memories come flooding back in one shot.

G: *But didn't you feel that she wasn't very good in the film?*
P: It was more complicated than that. We began a relationship during the shoot and she told me it was difficult for her to act in front of me as if nothing were going on between us, so I had to do a lot of takes.

G: *Do you think she could have become a great actress?*
P: Absolutely.

G: *You write in your book that she changed your life.*
P: Strangely enough, two or three weeks before her death, I thought to myself, "I'm so happy!" And suddenly I remember being afraid, as if it couldn't last.

G: *On 9 August 1969, when you were on top of the world, Sharon Tate was murdered in your Hollywood villa along with four other people by the Charles Manson family. She was eight months pregnant. You were in London.*
P: I was having difficulty writing a script called *Un animal doué de raison* and kept delaying my return trip to Los Angeles. The night before she died, Sharon and I spoke on the telephone, as we did every day, and I told her, "I'm coming home tomorrow."

G: *How did you cope with the trauma of her death?*
P: For months I couldn't think of anything else. I realize today I'm scarred for life.

G: *How have you changed since then?*
P: I can't enjoy myself as freely as I used to. I feel the same sense of Jewish guilt as my father did, and Sharon's death increases my belief in the absurd.

G: *Do you ever think of Manson?*

P: He doesn't mean anything to me. Let bygones be bygones. If Sharon had been killed in a car accident it would have been the same. The story's sensational side mattered most to the media who made a lot of money from it. It was a good source of profit for them. For me it was a tragedy.

G: *After the murder you tried to find the killers. In your book you write that you went so far as to suspect your best friends, including the singer of the group The Mamas and the Papas.*

P: I interviewed the people around him and one night even examined his Jaguar to see if there were any traces of blood. The police gave me the material to do it. And when Bruce Lee told me he'd lost his glasses, I suspected him. So I accompanied him to the opticians to see if his glasses matched those found in the villa after the crime. It just goes to show what paranoia can do to you.

G: *It was understandable behavior. After all, the press had no consideration for you, and in your book you rail against them.*

P: Why did they make us all out to be monsters? Before the culprits had been found the press made up all sorts of stories about drugs, orgies, and rituals, suggesting that the victims had brought this all upon themselves. The press effectively murdered them a second time.

G: *What is your own version of the events?*

P: The press blew the ritual aspect out of proportion and suddenly started playing Manson's game. The guy was not a first-time killer—he'd already spent a large part of his life in jail, but he assumed most of the attributes of the hippies, starting with his long hair and a Christ-like beard. He was also clever enough to have shrouded his crime behind an ideology—an evil one for sure—but which transformed it into a mythical event. Actually I think his motive was purely material: he wanted money and revenge. It was probably no coincidence that this frustrated artist sent his "family" to look for money in our house. Before we moved in Terry Melcher, a music producer who had rejected Manson's musical compositions, had been renting it.

G: *Why do you think the murders have taken on such mythic proportions?*
P: They sounded the death knell of the flailing hippie movement. Along with the Moon landings it's one of the events that marks the transition from the sixties to the seventies. Rather symbolic, don't you think?

G: *Did you return to the house after the killings?*
P: Only once afterwards. Never again.

G: *How did you manage to stay in Hollywood?*
P: When I left Hollywood after Manson's arrest I decided I'd never go back. Then I went to live in Rome and convinced myself that Europe was my homeland. My friends Jack Nicholson and Bob Evans, the Paramount producer, managed to persuade me to come back and make *Chinatown*. At the time I didn't have any plans or money. When I arrived in Los Angeles I realized that the screenplay wasn't ready yet. I took advantage of this to get the hell out of there. Every road I drove on brought the tragedy back to me. But I didn't have a choice—I had to make a living.

G: *How did the filming go?*
P: Bob Evans lent me a house in a neighborhood I wasn't familiar with. During the week I worked all day long on the film set without ever poking my head outside. At the weekend I threw parties. I left the day after we finished filming.

G: *The Krakow ghetto was not your fault, and nor were the Manson killings. But surely you brought the rape case upon yourself?*
P: It began when *Vogue Hommes* asked me to do something for them and I suggested a series of photos of teenage girls. Soon afterwards someone told me of a young girl who had the look I was after. She wanted to be a model and had already done some TV commercials. In my book I call her Sandra. While passing through Los Angeles to prepare a film, I went to see her.

G: *You took some photos of her on the Mulholland hills and then in Jack Nicholson's villa. You drank some champagne, you went for a swim in the pool, and then . . .*
P: I feel that you're uncomfortable asking your questions. But do go on.

G: *Do you regret having made love to this young girl?*
P: I regret everything I had to go through afterwards.

G: *She was thirteen years old.*
P: She was about to turn fourteen. Three weeks later to be exact.

G: *That's no excuse.*
P: If you had seen her, you would have thought she was at least eighteen years old.

G: *You pleaded guilty to statutory rape?*
P: So that the case could continue behind closed doors.

G: *Do you feel like the victim of a judiciary error?*
P: The young girl admitted in front of a tribunal that she'd already had intercourse with other people before meeting me, though the tribunal wasn't concerned about these other men. When Mr. Smith or Mr. Brown sleeps with fourteen year-old adolescents who look eighteen, it doesn't interest anyone. But when a famous film director does, the law and the press sound the alarm. It seems that I was the only one—or nearly the only one—to have found myself before a judge.

G: *You hit rock bottom when you were jailed for several weeks in Chino Californian penitentiary.*
P: Being in jail was an interesting experience. To be honest I found life as a convict fascinating. I got a much stronger understanding of why the people we call re-offenders, once released, look for new ways to get back behind bars. Since then, like those guys, I've found myself feeling nostalgic for the time I spent in there.

G: *That's masochism!*
P: What does a sailor miss when he finds himself back on dry land? The solitude and the rocking movement of the waves. Well, it's the same thing for an ex-con. He misses the boredom, the routine, the little dramas.

G: *You ended up leaving the United States. Does it upset you not being able to return?*

P: California is too removed from my own world. I'm basically European, and everything I love is here in Paris. I don't know of any other city in the world where you can see so much—all the exhibitions, films, concerts, fashion shows. But what makes me sad, naturally, is that France's creativity is not what it used to be. Each nation has its cycles, I think. Right now France is clearly on the crest of the wave. It's not talent that's lacking, more ambition.

G: *You have been chased by fate since your birth. Will there ever be any respite?*

P: I've always hoped so. I've always considered myself a nomad, but now I don't want to move anymore. I even find the idea of spending a weekend in the countryside unappealing.

G: *After all that you have gone through, you still look only thirty years old. What's your secret?*

P: My curiosity, without doubt. I'm always trying to learn something new. A language or a musical instrument. Old age is an illness that sets in when you don't want to learn anything new.

Polanski on Polanski

PIERRE-ANDRÉ BOUTANG/1986

WHAT SORT OF PERSON was the Pharaoh who built the biggest pyramids? A determined man, no doubt.

If you boast about your abilities, people say you're being arrogant, just like when Cassius Clay ran about chanting, "Dance like a butterfly, sting like a bee," and "I am the greatest, the fastest," over and over again.

Cinema is a battle, a war. At the moment of attack it's important to be absolutely certain that you're stronger than your enemy, that you can overrun the town, that you'll find food and drink and women there. No general would be able to lay siege to a town if one of his officers said to him that they "might" be able to take it. When I'm in the middle of making a film I have to be ready to deal with everything, and I psych myself up by running around shouting, "Dance like a butterfly, sting like a bee," at the top of my voice.

I pep myself up by telling myself that I'm the greatest, the most talented—a filmmaker of genius. When I'm working on a film, I truly believe it's going to be a success, and that's why I ask the people I'm working with to do all sorts of things I'd never usually ask of them.

You need more than just talent to make a film. You've got to have incredible energy when you're under that kind of pressure. Everyone's having a go at you, from the actor who has his own ideas about the character he's playing to the prop man who has problems, the producers who are worried about money, and the interviewers who want you

From *Polanski par Polanski*, Editions du Chêne, 1986. Reprinted by permission of Pierre-André Boutang. Translated by Paul Cronin and Remi Guillochon.

to be available for them, dutifully answering their questions, even when you're taking flack from all sides.

Filmmaking is about translating the ideas in your head to life. In this respect, it's the work of only one person—a one-man art form—because I'm the only person who knows what's going inside my head. If I listened to everyone's suggestions, the film would quickly become a meaningless mish-mash and I'd either have to abandon it mid-way or end up with a stomach ulcer. I find it difficult to be entirely satisfied with any solution to certain problems, and from this point of view I'm probably as ruthless as a producer.

People think I'm being objectionable when I insist that everyone should do exactly what I have in mind. But that would be masochism on my part. No one suffers more than the film director who's constantly struggling to get things done his way.

Often you know that something isn't as it should be, but you can't quite put your finger on what it is. You only know that something's missing—maybe a little detail which means the scene won't fit with the rest of the film.

The people around you can't understand why you're being so difficult, why you're shooting so many takes. After fifteen they start getting irritated. I wouldn't want to tell you what happens by the fifty-fifth.

Suppose, for example, you needed a shot of a man's fingers holding a cigarette. Some directors might do this in a couple of minutes. But the shot would actually be much more interesting if ash from the cigarette fell at a particular moment. And maybe it would look good if the lighting made the smoke hang in the air. Maybe put a table in the background with something on it—like a woman's hand holding a glass. Or maybe you want to see the floor where there's a dog playing. All these things should be tied in to the rest of the action. It takes only two seconds—a single meter of film—for tension to rise or fall. But it's not easy to get everything right in only fifty takes. I'm very aware of the cost of such things, but I really don't see this as perfectionism. It's just the absolute minimum that's required.

There's a Polish proverb: the better you make your bed, the longer you'll sleep. Producers don't like the fact that I'm meticulous, but every filmmaker who makes good films overspends just as much as I do. Maybe they're not as affected by it like I am, because every time it happens to me I get really upset. I can't sleep properly and my nerves are completely shot. I'd like to be able to say that I don't give a damn about things like going over budget, but it isn't so.

Filmmaking is all about sticking to your guns and refusing to compromise. A film is a dream, and to make that dream come true—even when it comes to a single shot—you must never concede anything to the money-men, the studio heads, or the schedule. At every stage of the process the director is surrounded by people whose interests run contrary to his own. A good director is one who makes only the tiniest concessions.

The problem is that you can't change your personality twice a day—at eight in the morning and seven-thirty in the evening, once the shooting's done. This becomes your way of life for a whole year—or even longer. When I finish a film and everything goes back to normal, it's always something of an anticlimax. I get the feeling that people hate me and that I've got so many enemies I need to get out of town as soon as possible.

If you were to look at me during shooting, you'd see my true nature. I take an interest in everything—not only in what's happening on the set but also everywhere else.

I don't need to say much to the technicians because we understand each other intuitively. I wouldn't have been a very good cameraman or a set decorator or sound engineer, even though I learned to do these jobs at film school and later on, when I started directing. I feel quite confident doing these jobs, and I'm able to suggest things to each person concerned without them feeling that I'm stepping on their toes.

Some directors get annoyed at everything—the crew, the equipment, the studio—but not me. The filmmaking process is like an enormous machine, bigger than a bulldozer, able to pick up hundreds of tons of earth just to get at two small stones. I don't really know anything about these machines, but when I look at the guy working the levers and removing these nuggets with such deftness and speed it reminds me of how I feel when things are running smoothly on the set.

I have the feeling that my crew is like an orchestra and I'm the conductor. When everything's working, we all feel part of a team.

Roman's Style

JEAN-PIERRE LAVOIGNAT AND
STELLA MOLITOR/1986

Q: *Do you have the feeling that you've achieved what you set out to do
with* Pirates?
A: It's hard to say right now because I'm still in the thick of it all.
Once I set myself certain goals I always end up reaching some of them.
It's hard to put into figures, but it's maybe 90 percent. That seems
about right. At least I think so, and I hope I'm not mistaken!

Q: *Can you define these goals?*
A: It's hard. Generally it means recreating an idea in your head in
a concrete form and making it accessible to others through the
extremely complex means of film production. If you add up all the
hours spent building things for the film and consider the hundreds of
people who've worked on *Pirates*, you can imagine the full extent of
what this means and the constraints they worked under. Everyone
works for the film, of course. But everyone also works in their own
interest.

Q: Pirates *is a project that you've wanted to make for ten years. Did your
desire ever wane during that time?*
A: Quite the opposite. It became almost an obsession, not only to
prove that I could do it but also because I was so keen on the idea.

From *Première*, May 1986. Reprinted by permission. Translated by Paul Cronin and Remi
Guillochon.

Each time I rewrote the screenplay and then reread it, I played out the characters and the scenes in my head, and realized I wanted to to see them on the screen. I was totally in love with them.

Q: *Did the screenplay change much over the ten years?*
A: It got a bit shorter. Four years ago, during one attempt to produce it, we decided to cut it a little. Back then the script was almost three hours long, and today it runs at two and a quarter hours.

Q: *You first pictured Jack Nicholson in the role of Captain Red. Did you have to change the character once Walter Matthau took on the role?*
A: Not really. The image I had of Captain Red hasn't changed. In any case, I'd always imagined someone older than Nicholson, whom I thought I could make look older by shaving his head. Straight after *Chinatown* I thought it would be interesting to make the film and give Jack the kind of role he'd never had before. But I think it frightened him a little.

Q: *Is that why he asked for so much money, which made his participation in the film impossible?*
A: That was certainly one of the reasons. I saw Jack not that long ago and we talked about the film again. He said to me, "I think I'm old enough now to play that sort of character." It was just after *Terms of Endearment*. Today I realize he was always reticent about something that wasn't to do with the role as such, which in itself was a lot of fun. It was more to do with the character. Actors are very vain and always prefer roles that please the ladies! In the end I think Walter Matthau was a better choice. Nicholson would have needed a make-over, and though I'm sure he would have played it very well, Matthau has a real presence as Captain Red.

Q: *When the film finally went into production, were you tempted to play the role of Frog?*
A: No. Each time I tried to start up the production I was conscious of the difficulties of being both actor and director. At the same time I modified the character a little bit. I was always in two minds about his comic and romantic sides, and finally thought it would be best

to have a young man with whom younger viewers could identify, someone romantic and a little less comic. Something of a heartthrob!

Q: *When you wrote the script, did you cut out certain scenes if you felt they might be too difficult to shoot?*
A: I didn't cut anything. The difficulty in putting the film together financially came from the fact that the story presented certain technical problems. During filming we never cut anything, even though it was an extremely complicated shoot, especially because of the continuity problems of shooting at sea. The color of the water changed and the sun would move from one side to the other. When I wrote the script with Gérard Brach we didn't set ourselves any limits. Having just made *Chinatown* put me in a good position to work on a big project without financial constraints, and I wanted to take advantage of this situation and make a film we both wanted to do. Gérard and I were in the mood to make an adventure film that would also be quite comical—an "entertainment" as the Americans say. When we began to look for a story, our starting point was the classic tales of swashbucklers and pirates. Then we created the characters and situations we wanted to see on screen.

Q: *Are you particularly keen on the world of pirates?*
A: Not really, but it does symbolize what the cinema was for me when I was a child. Ten years ago, before the success of films like *Star Wars*, there were practically no films like this. The success of *Star Wars* proved to me that the vast majority of the public want to see films like *Pirates* and that it would be popular with audiences. Today, however, the risk is that it appears somewhat less original than it did back then.

Q: *The hero in* Pirates *is called Captain Red. We can't help thinking of* Captain Blood, *the Michael Curtiz film with Errol Flynn.*
A: Yes, there's something to that. *Pirates* is something of a parody of the genre and in this respect is similar to *The Fearless Vampire Killers*. The characters are serious and the actors must be convincing, even if the situations they find themselves in are completely absurd.

Q: *Captain Red and Frog remind us of the Professor and the young man in* The Fearless Vampire Killers.

A: Yes, this was quite deliberate. Brach and I were in the same state of mind writing *Pirates* as we were for *The Fearless Vampire Killers*, though this wasn't so obvious during shooting. I remember the filming of *The Fearless Vampire Killers* as being a very happy time of my life, but on *Pirates* it was torture, a real nightmare.

Q: *Why?*

A: Because technically it was so difficult. The crew wasn't very cohesive—no more in nationality than in mentality. We were limited financially and were hardly spoilt by the weather. You know that the bigger a budget is, the more financial problems there are. I knew in advance that shooting would be difficult, but I never imagined it would be so slow. More and more problems sprang up which prevented us from doing our work. There was just too much interference for everything to fall into place at the right moments. It's easy to write "Captain Red, with his wooden leg stuck in the raft, hangs onto the galleon's rigging." But do you have any idea what this means when you break it down? You just want to drop it altogether! Of course, when audiences see it on the screen they accept it immediately. "Hey, there's the one-legged man up in the rigging!" But at the time we had to decide where to position the camera, where the galleon had to be in relation to where the sun was, and also find out how to keep the raft steady and where to put Matthau's real leg. That's to say nothing of the beard, the make-up, and the sound problems. And almost every shot was the same.

Q: *With all those problems, did you risk loosing sight of the film as a whole?*

A: With a film like this, the real challenge is to have a good idea of its make-up before shooting starts, even if one of the most important jobs of a filmmaker is to be able to anticipate changes and adapt to them. The problem is basically not to loose sight of your original concept during shooting, which isn't easy because reality never conforms exactly to the idea in your head. It gradually imposes itself onto your initial ideas and eventually completely erases it. My original conception of Captain Red clashed with the reality of the situation at hand.

The actor playing a part can never be perfect because you're dealing with a real person whose way of speaking and walking isn't precisely as you'd originally imagined. And the set direction—despite the endless discussions, meetings, and investigations—will also never be exactly as you dreamt it. There's always a discrepancy between dreams and reality. It's important to be open and able to see that new ideas can be just as good—maybe even better—than your original conception. But I think that if at the start of this project a prophet had told us we'd have to build a whole pirate ship, we wouldn't have written the script. And I say a prophet because I'd never have believed a producer if he'd told me.

Q: *So when you were writing the script with Gérard Brach you didn't think it would be so difficult to make?*
A: No, because at the start it *wasn't* difficult to make. When I finished the script all the studios were after us. It even worried me a little! I remember saying to my producer Andy Braunsberg, "It's going to be like when you're at a party with so many beautiful women that you don't know which one to go for, so you end up going home alone!" And that's exactly what happened!

Q: *Meaning?*
A: We were meant to do the film with an Italian producer/distributor. When the first budget was calculated we realized it was just too big for him, so I called Paramount as I'd worked with them before. They were interested and wanted to take over the project in its entirety, but we didn't want to do that out of loyalty to the Italian. This meant lots of problems and because of this we decided to drop Paramount. But when you abandon one studio, rumors start circulating and suddenly you find yourself acting like a plaintiff.

Q: *Pirates is the eighth film you've written with Gérard Brach. Such a longstanding partnership is a rare thing these days. What do you like the most about him?*
A: Who he is as a man, his human qualities. He's a friend and we understand each other perfectly and in very few words, which simplifies things.

Q: *How do you work together?*
A: Usually I have the initial ideas and he puts them into a more tangible form, then I return the shot. It's like ping-pong. He writes a scene and reads it to me, or I read it by myself and suggest some more or less significant changes which he makes. I reread it and so on until it reaches a form both of us are satisfied with. Often we begin by discussing and taking it in every possible direction. It's more like psychoanalysis. At a certain point—about a third of the way through the work—we begin to tackle the question of structure.

Q: *After* Tess *you called yourself an "ex-filmmaker."*
A: Yes. I just didn't want to make any more films. I found it all too disappointing. It required too much effort in areas that I didn't care for at all, like haggling and irritating meetings with finance people, lawyers, executives, agents. It meant devoting too much energy— maybe 80 percent—to things that had nothing to do with artistic creation, and only 20 percent on what you actually see on the screen. I remember working on my autobiography when the production head of Universal said he wanted to make a film with me. I told him, "I don't want to make any more films. I've just had enough of the headaches it all gives me." "But with us it won't be like that," he said. I believed him and told him about *Pirates* which was the only project that could possibly make me return to filmmaking. It was a project that I'd already began to discuss with producer Tarak Ben Ammar. I met Tarak through Claude Berri who loved the project and has done everything possible to bring the film to life. I also told Tarak that if *Pirates* was going to be as tough as *Tess* or even like the previous attempts to make the film, then it just wasn't worth it. Life really is too short for things like this. But both Universal and Tarak said it would be different, so we embarked upon this adventure full of hope and with the best intentions. In actual fact, because of the difficulties I've explained, it took a turn for the worst. [*laughter*]

Q: *Do you get the impression that your working methods have changed in the past ten years?*
A: Yes, inevitably. You change, you evolve. But in what way? It would be better to ask a psychoanalyst. [*laughter*] They say films are

expressions of the self. In fact, to answer your question more precisely, I think I'm more exacting of certain details, but I really haven't thought about it much.

Q: *If your films are the expression of your inner self,* Pirates *seems to reflect your childish side.*
A: Yes, doubtless. [*laughter*] Maybe getting older makes me more childlike.

Q: *But* Tess *and* The Tenant *were very tortured, dark, stormy films.*
A: Yes, but the screenplay of *Pirates* was written ten years ago.

Q: *Do you think that ten years later you can connect with the state of mind you were in when you wrote the original script?*
A: I don't think you can ever place yourself in the state of mind you had ten years previously, though you can feel nostalgic for it. In any case, I've never lost my childish side. Sometimes circumstances have forced me to be a little more serious or solemn, but as soon as I can allow it I've let myself be carried away by a careless spirit. I've always been a practical joker. I love to fool around, but certain things have happened to me that made me behave more seriously, including the way I express myself artistically. *The Fearless Vampire Killers* was the expression of that slightly childish state of mind. I made the film with my wife Sharon Tate and shortly afterwards she was murdered. I couldn't have made another film like *The Fearless Vampire Killers* straight after that—it would have been indecent. It was only ten years later that I could think about making *Pirates.*

Q: *Very few directors have changed their tone and style of films as much as you have. You've gone from comedy to drama, from fantasy to thriller.*
A: If I am eclectic it's because of my love for cinema. When I watch films—which is very often—it makes me want to remake whatever has really touched me. I want to re-create the pleasures I find there. This is where my desire comes from, nowhere else. You have to have seen and liked other films to want to make your own. I know there

are a lot of filmmakers who never go to the cinema, but I think what they really mean is that they used to go, just not anymore.

Q: *Is your favorite film also the one you think is the most accomplished?*
A: It's all relative. Normally I don't go back and watch my films, but I saw them all again when I wrote my book and that's when I realized that the one I really enjoyed seeing again was *The Fearless Vampire Killers*. It conjures up a very happy period of my life and I feel such warmth from the film. I was so happy to see it again from beginning to end, even if along the way I noticed some faults which I hope you can't. [*laughter*] Another film that gives me great satisfaction from a filmmaker's point-of-view is *Cul-de-sac*. I like its originality and style a lot. It has a truly cinematographic side. It's not theater, it's not a television program illustrated with slides—it's true cinema. From the point of view of the maturity of the cinematographic writing, another film is *Rosemary's Baby*. I think it's very well turned out without being overly polished, even if it's adapted from a book and has a pretty silly story. In the other films there are things I like alongside the errors, things I find embarrassing, scenes we botched and others that don't really work. There are things that seemed great at the time but which I find worthless today, and some weak acting along the way. Don't ask me which ones they are—I'm too ashamed to mention them. We try to avoid talking about our faults or errors, except to exorcise them, and I don't think I'm so guilty that I have to undergo that kind of suffering!

Q: *Aren't you a little afraid of going to Cannes with the bad memories you have of how* The Tenant *was received there?*
A: Yes, I was never that keen on going to Cannes, especially with a film like *The Tenant*. It wasn't made for the kind of audiences you find at Cannes, people who are inevitably conscious of everything that's going on. Cannes is a real battlefield, even if you're not in the competition. The concentration of envy and jealousy per square meter is so great that everyone's tolerance threshold is permanently exceeded.

Q: *Do you ever target any particular sections of the public with your films?*

A: I aim for the public at large, including children, and I'll target the children inside us all until until the day I die. Everyone makes films for the pleasure of seeing lines outside cinemas, and those who say otherwise are hypocrites. There's nothing more desperate than a forsaken life. It would certainly have been better if Van Gogh had sold more than one painting while he was alive.

Thriller *à la* Polanski

MICHEL PÉREZ / 1988

Q: Frantic *is a thriller which comes right after your pirate film. Are you making a point of trying out all the cinematic genres?*
A: I just make what I want to see on the screen. I'm like a waiter who serves food for himself. But actually I really never see anything too clearly because once a film is finished I'm always too involved to judge it properly. The reason I make genre films is because I really love cinema, and genre is what cinema is all about. I once said I was like a cinema playboy who wants to sleep with all the different genres: thrillers, musicals. There's one I haven't tackled yet: the Western.

Q: *What is the sexiest genre?*
A: Right now I think it's the thriller, but it changes all the time depending on what's going on around us, what we're all living through. We all move on and today I'm less interested in the films that I liked as a teenager when they affected me differently. No film made me happier than *Odd Man Out* by Carol Reed. Before that I was really into adventure films, *Robin Hood* and things like that. Since then I've understood that cinema has to make you feel you're in a secure universe with walls around you. It's not just about gaping at the hero.

Q: *And you decided to cast Robin Hood in* Frantic, *the original raider of the lost ark himself.*
A: Actually I saw Harrison Ford more in terms of his character from *Witness*. I could have asked Jeff Bridges or Kevin Costner to play the part.

From *Le Nouvel Observateur*, 25 March 1988. Reprinted by permission. Translated by Paul Cronin and Remi Guillochon.

I wanted an all-American boy: decent, upright, open, straightforward, physically strong, someone who could play "frantic" but who wasn't usually seen that way. I think Dustin Hoffman is one of the best actors around but I would never have asked him to take this role. The character in this film is someone with no real problems and who loves his wife, even if she is two years his senior and not particularly attractive. Being really in love with one's wife, being a family man—all this can be quite boring, and that's why more often than not we see the opposite on screen.

Q: *In the film the wife is the real love interest, not the dangerous blonde as might be expected. Is this because of new moral attitudes that are beginning to emerge in American films since the advent of AIDS?*
A: If I'd made this film ten years ago, I don't think there would have been any more physical contact between Harrison Ford and Emmanuelle Seigner, the girl he gets involved with. Of course my films, whether I like it or not, are a reflection of the society we live in. But the specter of AIDS had no bearing on the way Gérard Brach and I shaped the characters and it's not something I think will have any bearing on the stories I tell in the future. There have always been epidemics, like the bubonic plague that spread through urbanization. You could even say that social behavior has been shaped by diseases. Take the caste system in India. Those relationships are the result of long histories of infections. Ethnic groups who lived in different environments became a fatal danger to each other because they hadn't acquired immunity from the same viruses. We know the Spaniards didn't use brute force to vanquish the Aztecs—it was mainly through the influenza virus. All this is well documented in a book I've just read called *Plagues and Peoples*.

Q: *Are you concerned about what's happening in Israel?*
A: It's a pity that after twenty years they still haven't found a solution to their problems. Israel is losing its positive image. But I don't want to talk about politics, especially with regard to this film. I've tried to stay clear of politics as much as possible ever since I became disillusioned twenty-five years ago when living in Poland. I don't want to risk airing opinions that I might be ashamed of in years to come. Some people are too certain, too early about too many things. They're ready to sacrifice

their lives for what they believe are absolute certainties, and then later on—as is often the case—they realize they were wrong.

Q: *Your films seem to stay within the realm of fantasy and imagination.*
A: Fantasy? Not at all. *Frantic* is very much grounded in reality. There have been several attempts to smuggle a nuclear detonator—which plays an important part in the film—out of the United States into Israel. You could say that *Frantic* doesn't allow for a political interpretation—it simply shows how innocent ordinary folk can, at any time, fall victim to political intrigue. That's all.

Q: *It's a drama that disrupts the calm Parisian streets.*
A: From the start the idea was to make a film in the city where I live because I wanted to stay at home after being away for two years in Tunisia making *Pirates*. It had been a long time—not since *The Tenant*—that I'd shot a film there, and I wanted to show Paris to those Americans whose idea of the city is still based on *Irma la Douce* and *Moulin Rouge*. They seem to like it and are quite surprised to discover the Paris of the 1980s that serves as the story's backdrop.

Q: *What do you like about Paris?*
A: Everything, apart from the behavior of Parisians, the arrogance of the newspaper vendors, and the rude toilet attendants. I love the kind of energy that the city exudes. There's an ongoing renewal there—it's a living metropolis, not a museum. Places like Rome, Venice, and Amsterdam are beautiful cities but they smell of moth balls. Paris vibrates. You need five lives to keep up with what's going on. There are 350 films screened every week, more than you can find in any other city. For anyone interested in culture or who works in show business, it's heaven on earth.

Interview with Roman Polanski

MICHEL CIMENT AND MICHEL SINEUX / 1 9 8 8

Q: Pirates *took ten years to complete, but* Frantic *was much quicker.*
A: After having spent two years in Tunisia filming *Pirates*, I wanted to make a film quickly and, above all, without any beards, costumes, or galleons. A story set in Paris was exactly what I was after. After *Pirates*, Warner Bros. asked me if I had any other projects because they wanted to finance my next film. I said I wanted to do a thriller which immediately got them interested. They asked if I had a specific idea in mind, and I told them the story of an American who comes to Paris and whose wife goes missing. We signed a contract and all that was left was to write it, so of course I approached Gérard Brach.

Q: *It's a genre film, but at the same time you seem to want to explore the theme of American paranoia in the face of terrorism.*
A: At the time we were coming out of an intense phase of terrorism, and this idea of paranoia was in the air. But that wasn't the starting point for the film, which was simply the desire to make a thriller about a guy whose wife disappears. It's something that's been on my mind for a long time—this idea of someone who leaves for what seems to be a rather banal reason and never returns. We begin to ask ourselves questions: at what point should I start getting worried? You're in a restaurant, waiting for someone who has left to buy a packet of cigarettes

From *Positif*, May 1988. Permission granted by Michel Ciment. Translated by Paul Cronin and Remi Guillochon.

and who doesn't come back. After ten minutes it's already been a long time. After half an hour, what do you do? Do you carry on waiting? Almost immediately I think the worst and have nightmarish visions. Am I going to sit there for the whole day like an idiot? At what point do I pack my bags?

Q: *It deals with the disruption of daily life constantly looming on the horizon.*
A: Exactly. If it's a question of someone with whom you have an intimate connection, what do you do? What do you say to people? "She's gone but should have been back by now." It's unsettling for you, but not for anyone else. Later on in the film what appears to be the indifference of others is really just their manner—it's their way of getting on with everyday things—while the main character inevitably looks at things quite differently. There are probably a dozen cases like this every day.

Q: Chinatown *tells the story of a detective who takes on a case that doesn't concern him, but in* Frantic *the lead character—who could be compared to a private detective—is personally involved from the start. We're surprised you haven't been more tempted to make films about a character who sees everything from his own point of view.*
A: Actually I've always been interested in that idea, though theoretically I don't really want to make any more films like *Chinatown*, and practically speaking I haven't had the opportunity. As for subjectivity, I think what I wanted from the start was to film this guy who finds himself in lots of different places while the audience is looking over his shoulder. So it's a story that's more or less subjective, one I associate very much with the thriller genre.

Q: *Why did you want the character to be a doctor?*
A: That came afterwards. We'd thought about a couple on their honeymoon but I felt it would be better to find a more concrete reason for them to be in Paris other than for pleasure. That's how we came to this idea of the doctor at a conference.

Q: *But you retained the honeymoon idea.*
A: Yes, it's a remnant. It seemed a good idea that they'd been to Paris once before and that the wife speaks a bit of French. At one point we

explored the possibilities of the wife but realized we really didn't have time to go into their relationship and at the same time show his search for her once she goes missing. We came back to the wife and tried to write some scenes that would sketch out their relationship, but it was better that she just disappeared immediately.

Q: *The start of the film is like a romance as they sing "I Love Paris" in the shower together.*
A: They're just a couple of everyday Americans who come to Paris. That's the kind of thing they'd do.

Q: *Does your collaboration with Gérard Brach stem from similar ideas about cinema?*
A: There's no real method—it's more that we've developed a kind of routine. I explain the theme and we discuss it together, and then steadily improve on things. Little by little a sequence is created which seems worth putting to paper, and that's when Gérard starts to write. He reads me what he's written and we discuss it again. I often play out the parts, miming the situations and moving around a lot.

Q: *You don't actually write yourself?*
A: I used to a few years ago, but not anymore.

Q: *One of the starting points of* Frantic *is that the lead character doesn't speak French.*
A: We tried to create as many situations that could result from this, as it helped push the action forward and added an air of mystery to the story. There were quite a few scenes like this that we ended up cutting—for example another scene with the tramps—because it was becoming too much of a cliché. I wanted to get rid of everything that was too obviously quaintly Parisian and tried to show the city of today—the way I see it and not as Americans might imagine it to be. As Gérard Brach doesn't speak the language very well, contrary to our usual working method I asked him to write some things in English which I felt would add a certain authenticity to Harrison Ford's character.

Q: *In your two films that are set in Paris*—The Tenant *and* Frantic—*the image you give of the city is, to say the least, hostile.*

A: Let's just say I've felt some hostility around me in Paris. Not today but certainly in the 1950s when I lived there. *The Tenant* was based on Roland Topor's novel, though the hostility in the story was exaggerated through the main character's paranoia. We don't know if the tension around him is real or imagined. Actually I really don't think there's that much of a sense of hostility in *Frantic*. I think the film shows the city as it really is: self-absorbed and indifferent. Nothing's that exaggerated—I think it's an honest portrayal of Paris. The people that the doctor meets don't seem, to me at least, to be hostile or indifferent. They listen to his problems, but what can they do? Of course, the hotel detective is incompetent, but that's how those men are. I've met several of these people—they're often ex-policemen who have become head of security in hotels. Not very astute people.

Q: *Some scenes—for example where he's forcefully carted off—remind us of your other films: Rosemary being locked in* Rosemary's Baby, *Jack Nicholson in* Chinatown *forced up against a fence and threatened at knife-point by a sadistic killer, scenes that are filmed in a much more subjective way.*

A: I wish there were more scenes like that in *Frantic*, but the direction of the story doesn't always permit it. The rule in a film like this is just to put the hero in as much difficulty as possible.

Q: *There seems to be a real consistency in your work in that everything is seen from the point of view of the main character. Look at* Repulsion, Rosemary's Baby, Chinatown, The Tenant, *and* Frantic. *How does this approach affect the* mise-en-scène?

A: It doesn't only affect the *mise-en-scène* but also the screenplay where everything is laid down and which is the instruction manual to the film. The *mise-en-scène* is nothing other than the execution of the screenplay. When I write a script I always know where I'm going to put the camera later on.

Q: *So for you the* mise-en-scène *begins with the screenplay?*

A: I think it's like that for everyone.

Q: *Do you storyboard the action?*

A: No, only when I need to communicate things to the technicians that are hard to explain verbally, like special effects. I had a fairly precise series of storyboards for *Pirates* but generally I try to avoid this because it constrains the actors. The unavoidable clash with reality during filming shows that storyboarding isn't always an option.

Q: *What part does improvisation play in your approach to filmmaking?*

A: Improvisation is useful when positioning actors in particular places, delivering dialogue and filming scenes in certain ways. I begin rehearsing with the actors and then decide how I'm going to shoot the scene, never the other way round. That's why I don't like using storyboards.

Q: *Let's use the example of the first scene in the hotel room. Was it prepared in advance or was it improvised on location?*

A: No, it wasn't prepared and I didn't know how I was going to position the actors before we got in there. I let them come in just as people would normally arrive in a hotel and had them behave instinctively. Then I moved them around for the benefit of the camera. All I knew is that I needed time to prepare because I wanted some depth of field to the shot, something that's useful when creating the state of anxiety that builds up during the first twenty minutes of the film. Everything seems normal but the audience still gets worried. Or at least I hope it does.

Q: *Do you have particular actors in mind when writing a script?*

A: No, not at all. We didn't know if this character was going to be a doctor and we weren't even sure what was in the suitcase. I was looking for a motive for the kidnapping and thought that the mixing-up of suitcases was the answer. For a time we thought of drugs but that seemed rather banal, so I looked for another kind of valuable object. Then I remembered the story of kryton that the American media were talking about three years ago. Initially we didn't know what kind of character we were dealing with, and when we decided to make him a doctor we had to decide what kind of doctor. Was he a nervous Dustin Hoffman-type, someone I thought about for the role? But when writing the script we realized the character was less complicated and more robust. That's not to say that Dustin Hoffman isn't robust, but what we needed was an "all-American boy"—Harrison Ford or Jeff Bridges or Kevin Costner.

Q: *Or Cary Grant.*
A: Yes, exactly. The character is more Cary Grant than Jimmy Stewart.

Q: *It was also important that nothing happened between him and Michelle.*
A: Yes. I knew instinctively that Harrison would be good for the role. I met him when I was working on a script with his wife, Melissa Mathison. I told him I was writing another script with Gérard Brach and asked him what he was working on. He told me that the scripts he'd been reading weren't interesting and that he didn't know what he was going to do next. At my home one day I explained the story to him for two and a half hours after which Harrison said, "I'm happy because I don't have to read any more scripts." Of course Warner Bros. were enthusiastic because we'd chosen our central character and from that moment on we could move very quickly. Before that we were in two minds. Who was this guy? Would he be cool, reserved, or nervous? Now I could ask Harrison about all these little details—razors, shoes, etc. I phoned him and asked, "Harrison, would you set your watch on the plane or at the hotel?"

Q: *It's the first time jet lag has been represented like this on screen.*
A: I know the feeling—arriving at the hotel in the morning, the pleasure in taking a bath, of winding down and reading the newspaper. Should I sleep now or wait until later? I wanted to show all these kinds of things, and I'm glad you picked up on them.

Q: *The fact that he's a surgeon allows you a dramatic contradiction. He feels belittled and isolated because he can't speak French, yet he has a lot of common sense and is able to cope very well.*
A: This was Harrison's idea. He told me, "Heart surgeons are very meticulous people who do things in set ways." We researched this together and I spoke to quite a few doctors including Carpentier, one of the inventors of the artificial heart.

Q: *The paradox is that we never actually see him practicing his craft.*
All the same, was it useful in establishing his character?
A: When you meet lots of surgeons you notice they all have something in common. When you invent a character, you always ask yourself how he'll behave—if he'll do such and such a thing—and if you see
someone actually behaving like that, you feel more confident of your
creation.

Q: *The surgeon doesn't evolve very much throughout the film, as opposed to*
Michelle, most obviously her wardrobe.
A: I know this kind of woman, though in real life Emmanuelle
Seigner is the opposite of her character. She's much more innocent and
naïve. Emmanuelle started to dress like her character during the shoot
because she found it fun, but shed Michelle's skin as soon as filming
was over. The inspiration for Michelle was a photo taken by one of
Emmanuelle's friends in the subway where she's wearing a thuggish-
looking leather jacket. Nightclubs are full of people like this. Anthony
Powell, the costume designer, later came up with a completely different
design. I told him it wasn't quite right so he started exploring in the
direction of the photograph.

As far as the red dress goes, we started with the doctor's wife because
when he's looking for her I wanted him to be able to say, "She's
wearing a red dress." I wanted something very noticeable. When he's
in the shower we see she's wearing red. I was in town one day with
Emmanuelle who wanted to buy some clothes. I really don't like shopping with people and was waiting for her to one side when suddenly I
noticed a red dress on display and said to myself, "My God, what if
Michelle is also wearing a red dress at the end of the film? We find that
both women are wearing a red dress." So I asked Emmanuelle to try it
on—it's the one she ends up wearing in the film. It's very attractive in
an elegant and sexy way.

Q: *This corresponds to the film's color scheme. It starts with beige and grey.*
A: Just grey, no beige. At the beginning the décor in the hotel was all
beige, as in the Grand Hotel. Then three days into filming I said to
myself, "This isn't right. It has to be monochromatic. We need to paint
everything grey." I spoke to production designer Pierre Guffroy who

immediately understood. But the producer got wind of this and kicked up a fuss.

Q: *It creates an usual effect because Ford's character ends up leaving the protected, comfortable, and colorless hotel, but outside Paris is quite menacing with its aggressive coloring. It seems you wanted to depict a somber Paris. Why?*
A: I didn't want a colorful Paris like you see in American films. I wanted it to be grey, but with certain aspects exaggerated, like the green of the Mayor's city and the garbage men's outfits.

Q: *How important are the sound effects and music in your films? A memorable scene in* Repulsion *was created almost solely through a cleverly balanced mixture of silence and noise, and the effect that this has on the heroine's sister who is making love in the next door room.*
A: During filming I don't think about music, except for certain specific scenes where it's clear I need a particular type of music. In these cases I even explain to the actors what music there will be as it suggests a mood for them to aim for. Most of the time I take an interest in music and the composer only once a film is finished. We decide what we need and where it should go, though with *Frantic* I talked to the composer Ennio Morricone before I started shooting. Ennio doesn't speak English so instead of translating the script I told him the story in Italian. When he arrived after the filming had finished he already had a good idea of the music he wanted to use. It was based on both an electronic structure and a thematic one that would fit into the electronic framework, one we could change and replace if we wanted. Once the filming was done, I did actually change the music completely.

For the sound editing we prepared all the effects and then made the final decisions. The sound editor will often prepare more than I actually need, though for *Frantic* it was less than usual because I explained to him exactly what was necessary. I didn't want a very extensive sound-track and even the technicians were surprised that I didn't want to use more street noises. I wanted something quieter, and much of the film's suspense comes from the use of sound. It's a question of balance, but it's as difficult to explain as to bake a pie. Every cook uses the same ingredients but some end up with better pies than others. It comes down to proportion.

Q: *Your films, particularly this one, give the impression of realism, even though everything is actually stylized.*
A: I shoot in studios because it's more practical to do so. I can get better results and it's usually less expensive, though for the gymnasium scene in *Frantic* it made no sense to re-create it. The owner is a friend of mine and we shot only one sequence there. The idea was to make a film about the things I know—to show *my* Paris, as I consider it to be very much my town. Shooting in places that I'm familiar with gave me the opportunity to focus on the more interesting things the city has to offer. On the other hand, The Blue Parrot nightclub was filmed entirely in a studio and is a faithful re-creation of Les Bains-Douches. This really amused the set decorators who had to copy every nook and cranny. When the owner and clientele of the real club came to visit they were completely disorientated. We'd changed the layout of the place because Les Bains-Douches is spread over two floors, but we didn't have time to re-create the discotheque on another floor so we put it behind the bar instead. I also wanted to shoot with real people and knew we could only do it once. The next time they wouldn't come back as extras because by then they would be bored by it all. We could never have filmed in a single day at the real Bains-Douches, but building a set didn't actually cost much more because if we'd used the real place we would have had to compensate the owner, place illegally parked cars to prevent other cars from parking, bring in wardrobes for the actors and install a generator for the lights. So in this case filming in a studio was more economical. We could take down the walls and the ceilings easily, and all the lights were already in place.

Q: *Betty Buckley was an interesting choice for the role of Harrison Ford's wife.*
A: You've seen her in *Tender Mercies* and *Carrie,* and she's also a singer who has appeared in *Cats* and *The Mystery of Edwin Drood.* She wasn't an obvious choice. I was about to make the mistake of choosing someone sexier for the role. We were trying to find a way of making the audience identify with a character who disappears very quickly and realized we needed a woman who was above all likeable and maternal.

It would be someone the doctor met during his studies and with whom he's raised a family. I began to think of people I know in Los Angeles—doctors and lawyers who resemble these characters. My lawyer, for example, who has become a good friend, is an Olympic swimmer, a big and healthy handsome guy who lives with his wife and three children. They are a couple who truly love each other a lot. I can't imagine one without the other. I thought it would be easier for the audience to understand what this man is going through if he were married to this kind of woman.

Q: *With a thriller, audiences often know what's going to happen next. They are one step ahead of the characters but are no less frightened, and sometimes don't know any more than the characters themselves.*

A: We made a big effort in *Frantic* for the audience not to outsmart Harrison Ford. If the characters on screen know less than the audience, they tend to look foolish. We can't help but ask ourselves: why doesn't he do this or that? Why doesn't he see what I see? So we tried to make Harrison Ford's character intelligent enough so he understands things as quickly as the audience does. Another possibility is that of the super-smart policeman who understands everything in advance and leaves the audience behind, then explains in lengthy tirades what's actually happening. We didn't want that either. If we've managed to keep the same level of information on both sides, then we've succeeded in what we wanted.

Q: *Did you always have that ending in mind? It seems more traditional and less surprising than the rest of the film.*

A: It was a bit different to begin with. Quite honestly I was never very happy with the ending. I asked myself if maybe it should be a bit more out of the ordinary.

Q: *One wonders if you wanted to recapture the climax of* Cul-de-sac *which makes a mockery of all those clownish characters.*

A: I wanted to show the characters moving around the suitcase, this utterly insignificant object. It's got absolutely nothing to do with the three people in the film and yet is the cause of the girl's death and the couple's sufferings. The original ending had Harrison Ford escaping and

finding himself in a taxi stuck in traffic, whereupon he discovers
the krytron in his pocket. We filmed all of this but it was even longer
than the ending we used.

Q: *It seems to come straight out of the theater of the absurd.*
A: It may well be that I'm still influenced by things I liked when I
was younger. I'm slowly shedding these influences, but some things
die hard!

Q: *You're very attached to the theater, both as director and an actor. Has
your time spent there enriched your work as a film director?*
A: It's given me a lot of insight, yes. Of course it's difficult to unravel
the many layers of influences over the years and say which come
from the theater and which from elsewhere. But it helps me enormously
that the two forms—theater and cinema—resemble one another. My
experiences as an actor have clarified certain things and helped me in
my work with actors when I'm on a film set. Inevitably I have a better
understanding of some of their problems.

Q: *Why did you choose to play Gregor Samsa in the stage version of
Kafka's* Metamorphosis?
A: There was no reason other than wanting to be back onstage. I like
to play roles that have a physical dimension and which are a real challenge, otherwise I get bored. I didn't have time to direct it—I only
wanted to act in it. Most of the time I'm not offered interesting things,
but *Metamorphosis* really appealed to me and I knew I could handle it.

Q: *How did you approach the role of someone who is part-insect and
part-human?*
A: It's a mechanical process. At the beginning I didn't know what to
do at all, but with a lot of practice and study, the role started to make
sense. It was a bit like Kafka's *In the Penal Colony*. I watched Steven
Berkoff, the director, demonstrating all the movements until I began to
understand what playing the character entailed, including his relationship with his family and his alienation from them. In all honesty it was
only the day before opening night that I really started understanding
how to play it.

Q: *The play reminded us of your first short films.*

A: *The Fat and the Lean* and *Mammals*, yes. When I was doing preproduction on those films I played all the characters myself. Once I'd found the right actors, I showed them what I wanted, just as a conductor plays a note to an orchestra member. He doesn't know how to sing the note himself yet still manages to get his message across.

Q: *Whereas you are, in fact, an actor.*

A: Yes, but when I show the actors what I want I never do it very well. I'm never absolutely certain what I want and never make that great an effort to demonstrate because if a director acts something out too well he can put the actor off. If he acts it badly, on the other hand, the actor still understands what the director wants but will improve on the technique.

Q: *Kafka must have meant a lot to you when you were young.*

A: A great deal, especially as I came across him during one of the worst periods of Stalinism in Poland when only state literature was available. The Polish translations of Kafka were destroyed and weren't reprinted. I was a member of a small library that had held onto many books from before the war. The first one I got my hands on was *Ferdydurke* by Gombrowicz. I was utterly charmed by it because I didn't know this kind of literature even existed. Then I discovered Bruno Schultz's *Cinnamon Shops* and heard about Kafka. I read *The Trial* and realized there was something else out there. It was as if I had discovered masturbation. No one was going to stop me! Then at art school I studied things most people of my age didn't know anything about, like Impressionism, Cubism, Dada, and Surrealism. These were good times for us—like the discovery of sex in the Victorian Era.

Q: *Frantic is a magisterial exercise of genre filmmaking. But you've always spoken of* Cul-de-sac *as being your favorite film. Would you like to make another non-genre film?*

A: I know I want to do something new but don't know exactly what. As we say in Polish, "I hear the bells ringing, but I don't know from which church they're coming."

Being Merciless

GERHARD MIDDING / 1990

M: *When you see your old films today, do they live up to your current standards? What do you think of* Rosemary's Baby *for example?*
P: I find that there are lots of things in my work I don't like anymore, but this isn't the case with *Rosemary's Baby* which I feel is told very fluently and which I'm not embarrassed to watch today. It was based on a novel so I don't feel so responsible for the storyline. But overall it's a good production: well acted and edited. In fact, it's the first of my films that I feel is almost perfectly edited. That's thanks to the editor Sam O'Steen with whom I worked for the first time. He taught me to be merciless, to separate myself from scenes that might be good but that have no place in the finished product.

Another film I don't find unpleasant to watch today is *The Fearless Vampire Killers*. It's an easygoing and unpretentious film. Luckily the director didn't take himself too seriously.

M: What? *was a critical failure. What do you think of the film today?*
P: I haven't seen it since we made it, sixteen or seventeen years ago. My impression at the time was that I hadn't done justice to the script. When Gérard Brach and I finished writing it, we had the feeling of having done something extraordinary. The screenplay was witty, but when I saw the film something was missing. I'd just made too many

From *Die Tageszeitung*, 11 August 1990. Reprinted by permission of Gerhard Midding. Translated by Tamara Kraljic and Paul Cronin.

mistakes and it didn't quite express what we were trying to say. But it might be interesting to see how the film has aged. Maybe I should look at it again.

M: *Your filmography gives the impression that you have tried to work with a number of different genres, though you do seem to be particularly keen on fantasy films.*

P: Not really. The first fantasy film I made was *The Fearless Vampire Killers* which was actually a parody of the genre. *Knife in the Water* clearly wasn't fantasy and *Repulsion*, which is about the dreams of the main character, was maybe on the borderline. Do I have an affinity for the fantasy film? I don't know.

How does a filmmaker decide to make a film? In this respect I'm very often inspired by what I've just seen in the cinema. I've always loved going to the movies, today just as much as when I was younger. Gérard Brach and I saw an awful lot of films in the little student cinemas in St. Germain-des-Près in Paris, where we were daily visitors. At the time there were a lot of Hammer horror films playing, and Gérard and I discovered that the scarier a scene was, the more the audience laughed. I remember one time after a film suggesting we make a movie that would be intentionally funny. After *Repulsion* and *Cul-de-sac*, both of which were successful enough to give us some credibility as filmmakers, we felt ready to go out and try it. People would have laughed at us before.

M: *It's interesting that even in your horror and fantasy films, you place a lot of emphasis on the audiences' identification with the main character, for example* Repulsion *where you lead the viewer deeper and deeper into Carole's neurosis.*

P: The viewer's identification with the main character is essential, no matter who he or she is. Without this identification the viewer will lose interest in the film. Of course there are some characters who can be looked at from a distance, but that's boring, don't you think? In a film about neurosis there should be some identification—some sympathy— with the heroine, despite everything she does. *Repulsion* seems to speak particularly to women. It was much more popular than I expected when it was released, something due mainly to female audiences.

What's especially important is telling a story in the most realistic way possible. A character's actions must be motivated in such a way that the audience can understand what's happening, and this is especially true for horror and fantasy films. Or, to quote an appropriate literary example, Kafka's stories are fantasy yet his writing style is of such incredible realism that the reader has to pause for a moment and ask himself, "Can this really be happening?"

M: Repulsion *is also a remarkable picture of London in the early sixties. What do you pay attention to when shooting in foreign locations?*
P: A film has to be rooted in reality if it's going to convince anyone, or at least in some aspects of reality. When you set a film like *The Fearless Vampire Killers* in Transylvania, you have to invent the location—the scenery, the culture, the costumes, and traditions. But when a film is set in modern-day London it's much easier because you can just look around you. I made *Repulsion* during my first stay in the city, and when you're in a new place for the first time you notice all the little differences. Not just the language, everyday things too—like light switches and street signs. These kinds of observations can be very inspiring. When I first saw those buskers, for example, I immediately knew I wanted to put them in the film.

M: *Does* Rosemary's Baby *better reflect American society than* Chinatown, *which you made after living for a while in the United States?*
P: Yes, I would say so. At the beginning you're much more receptive, you notice things that later you take for granted because you're so used to them. If a director is able to reconstruct these things on film, the results can be exciting. I think *Rosemary's Baby* is pretty American, but neither that film nor *Chinatown* have any major mistakes or misconceptions. However, had the dialogue in *Rosemary's Baby* been more important to me, it certainly would have been better to have spent more time in America. As it happens, most of the dialogue was taken straight from the novel.

M: *You and Gérard Brach have collaborated on very different material and genres over the years. How do the two of you work together?*
P: It varies according to what project we're working on. With *Frantic*, for instance, we started by simply sitting together and talking. These

discussions often have no bearing on the script at all, though there are always a few things that stay in the back of our minds. When I get the feeling we've done enough talking I ask him to write a scene. It doesn't necessarily have to be the first one—it can be any scene. Then he reads it to me and I get new ideas and we rewrite, not necessarily to consolidate things but to make them less contrived. Often we rewrite a scene ten or twenty times. In the beginning I had to motivate Gérard to get to work, but today he does it out of habit.

There's nothing worse than a blank page. But once we start writing there's something to work with, and we're able to put the pieces together step by step. In most cases I'm in charge of the construction, something that comes easily to me as a director. Gérard is better with dialogue and the atmosphere of a particular scene. He has a very creative mind, most of the time coming up with more material than we actually need. It's a shame as he often writes very beautiful scenes that don't find their way into the finished films.

M: *Why are so many of your films told in the form of a circle?*
P: The entire composition, not only individual scenes, is of the utmost importance. The rondo often seems to me an appropriate narrative form. It invites you to reflect, at the end, on your starting point.

M: *I'd like to ask you about Robert Towne who wrote* Chinatown *and who helped you with the script of* Frantic.
P: He helped me in the last stage of *Frantic*. I always had a good relationship with Bob, despite the regular fights we had. I hope our paths will cross again in the future.

M: *Towne's reputation as a script doctor is legendary. It's an open secret that he worked on* The Godfather *and* Bonnie and Clyde. *What changes did he make on* Frantic?
P: When you work day in and day out on the same film, it becomes very hard to tell who did what. The contributions and ideas of the people participating in the process overlap, so I can't answer your questions precisely.

I sent Bob the script and asked him to tell me what he thought. He had a few suggestions that improved it, and I told the people at Warner

Bros. that he could enrich the script enormously. He came to Paris for a few weeks and we talked. In particular he added a few very witty and intelligent pieces of dialogue. I remember discussing the opening scenes in the hotel in particular, though his contribution is spread throughout the script. Bob cut out quite a lot because he could see things with a fresh eye. He noticed a lot of things that didn't seem obvious to us because I knew the story so well and couldn't look at it objectively.

M: *You cast the supporting roles in* Frantic *particularly well, especially the hotel staff who are polite yet exude a sense of danger.*
P: The supporting cast of a film is extremely important to me and I always spend a great deal of time casting them. I watch a lot of videotapes of actors who've been chosen by the casting director and meet dozens of people who I could imagine playing the role. Every single aspect of filmmaking is important—nothing can be neglected. It's like painting a picture. Look at this Archimbaldo on the wall. For him, every single centimeter of the painting was important. Many important elements of a film are noticed by audiences only if they're done badly.

M: *You have acted in a lot of your own films. How do you handle both roles?*
P: I often have problems when directing myself because the actor in me is such a temperamental character! In fact, I find working as a director much easier. Directing means putting things in the right place, giving orders, keeping an eye on everything. Acting required a lot of concentration. But when, as an actor, I see my fellow actors aren't standing in exactly the right place or that there's a shadow on a face that shouldn't be there, I get distracted and lose my concentration.

M: *How did this fit with the two directors who have acted in your own films, John Huston and John Cassavetes.*
P: With Huston, who assumed his role *Chinatown* perfectly, it was definitely easier. He looked like one of those businessmen from Texas or California who live on a ranch and breed horses. They're very different from European businessmen. John did his thing very well and it was a pleasure to work with him. He didn't have any problems with me

telling him what to do and was happy to accept my direction. He was big enough not to have any complexes about what he was doing. My experience with Cassavetes on *Rosemary's Baby* was completely different though.

M: *What inspired you to play the lead in* The Tenant*?*
P: At that point I was working with Paramount and they had the rights to the Roland Topor novel. I thought it would be a good role for me. As a matter of fact, I found it more interesting to play the part than to direct the film. I find this with a lot of scripts, and it's actually rare that both things appeal to me at the same time. You shouldn't forget that I started as an actor and only became a director later.

M: *Have there been parts in films made by other directors you would have liked to play?*
P: Yes, there were a few. I get a lot of these kinds of offers but I won't name the films. Sometimes I use my other commitments as an excuse because I'm scared to work with people I don't know. I also feel that life is too short for me to throw myself into projects that aren't my own. But I will tell you about one part that was offered to me. A long time ago Steven Spielberg offered me a role in his first Indiana Jones film as the Nazi officer, the one who burns his hand. Unfortunately I was busy and couldn't make it to Tunisia, the place where the film was shot, which was a shame because I would have found out just how chaotic it is to shoot there. A few years later I ended up filming *Pirates* in Tunisia.

M: *Would you have accepted the role?*
P: I really wanted to work with Steven Spielberg.

M: *There are always rumors about projects you're working on. Mickey Rourke, for instance, announced you were going to make a film with him.*
P: That project appealed to me only because of Mickey Rourke, but when I gave it some thought I realized it wasn't for me. In any case, I'd simply agreed to read the script and meet Rourke. Producers always have a habit of informing the public and the press a little too prematurely.

M: *Is it true you're in the running for the main role in the film version of Patrick Süskind's novel* Perfume?

P: They haven't asked me to act in it—they want me to direct. Claude Berri, the producer, told me about the book when it came out and I also met with the author. But I've never seriously thought of making it, despite the fact that I think there's a film in there somewhere.

M: *I assume that the rumors about you making a film about the life of Lech Walesa aren't true.*

P: There's a photograph of him with Robert de Niro and me taken during a visit to Gdansk. It was nothing more than that, though I think his life has the makings of a damned fine film.

M: *Considering the changing situation in Eastern Europe, would you like to shoot a film in Poland?*

P: I've been to Poland quite often in the past few years, and eight years ago I acted in a play there. But you mustn't forget that the events of late happened so quickly, that things spun out of control in East Germany, Romania, and Czechoslovakia. In Poland, the process has been going on for years. I'd very much like to make a film there, but the film industry is in a miserable state. On the technical side they're far worse off than in Czechoslovakia, for example.

M: *I gather you're currently preparing a script for Warner Bros.*

P: Yes. It's from a book called *Mary Reilly*, written by an American, Valerie Martin. I was sent the final draft together with some other scripts from Warner Bros. and thought it looked interesting. It's going to be a studio film, or as it's called in France, a *film de commande*. It's not a project that I initiated myself, but I think the material's exciting and I'm currently rewriting the script.

M: *What kind of story is it?*

P: It's a fantasy, but under no circumstances will I tell you anything more. The book will be out sometime this year.

Interview with Roman Polanski

ANTOINE DE BAECQUE AND
THIERRY JOUSSE/1992

Q: *Did you plan to leave Poland after making your first films at the Lodz film school?*
A: I never saw my career developing in Poland. "Go West" very quickly became a necessity for me. To begin with, Poland's borders have always been a place of considerable uncertainty—halfway between the concentration camp and those parts of the country laid waste during the war. It wasn't a place where you could reasonably grow up. In fact I didn't grow up there. I "lived" there—let's say I survived—until I was twenty years old when I quickly became an adult. I was an adult in a child's body, a hyphenated being, an "adult-child." There was nothing between the two, nothing you would usually associate with childhood, like an education or an upbringing. Amongst my contemporaries there weren't many "young and ambitious" people—as they were called with some suspicion—who planned to stay Poland. On the other hand, it wasn't like this at all for the generation that immediately preceded us, for example Andrzej Wajda who very quickly symbolized the New Polish school and who—even if the regime was sometimes suspicious of him—was able to put together certain working facilities there. But for us it was the opposite. Poland was a cramped and unpleasant country, and cinema had no future there.

From *Cahiers du Cinéma*, May 1992. © *Cahiers du Cinéma*. Reprinted by permission. Translated by Paul Cronin and Remi Guillochon.

Q: *So your dream and frame of reference lay in America?*
A: It was more France. My parents loved Paris, I was conceived and born there, and my mother and father often spoke about the country during the war. It was like a dream, a world away from the war. During our education in Lodz we were able to see lots of French films, works by Clément, Autant-Lara, and Clouzot, and all the prize-winners from Cannes like *The Four Hundred Blows*.

Q: *You said "our education"?*
A: I'm thinking of Skolimowski as well. He's an odd but rather endearing friend from even before school. He was a Bohemian poet, ran a jazz group, and was an amateur boxer who started to write scripts with Wajda, then me, including *Knife in the Water*.

Q: *At this time the school in Lodz seems to have been a stimulating place to be.*
A: Stimulating isn't the word. We lived in a very strict country and the school was a place of privilege where the students, who had a real thirst for learning, also enjoyed certain freedoms. Don't forget that Lenin said cinema was the most important art form that existed, something that gave a lot of prestige to filmmakers. This meant the Communists didn't dare interfere with us too much. The school's reputation was one of having reinvigorated young Polish cinema. It was a relaxed and artistic environment where we could talk openly about things most people kept to themselves—a bit like the seminary priests who make jokes about God and the Virgin Mary. We were also able to keep in touch with Western culture since the censor allowed us "specialists" to see a lot of American, Italian, and French films. But what really counted was the high level of technical training. Lodz was a place where you could learn a profession, and on leaving we really knew how to make films. It was a bit like the VGIK [Russian State Institute of Cinematography] in Moscow, a very professional school that was inspired by Hollywood and where training and practical experience was the key.

Q: *What seems paradoxical is that you wanted to leave Poland at the time when everyone was talking about the new wave of Polish directors and when all the film journals of the early 1960s—like* Positif *and* Cahiers du

Cinéma—*were telling us that Poland was a place to watch. In fact you left while others like Skolimowski, Forman in Czechoslovkia, Makavejev in Yugoslavia, and Jancso in Hungary all stayed to take advantage of the movements that were taking shape.*

A: I've always considered myself to be cosmopolitan—not tied down to any particular place. To the Poles I was ever so slightly French and in the West I was always considered Polish. In fact, even if I did benefit from being pigeonholed like other young European filmmakers of the 1960s, I never really belonged to those groups. I just didn't need to be tied down that way. Let's say my strength—or my opportunism—was to have sensed these currents before most other people did. What Forman, Skolimowski, and then all the others ended up doing was to go and explore elsewhere, something I did much earlier. So early, in fact, that I was nearly expelled from film school on several occasions.

The outgoing students from Lodz were very much influenced by Soviet cinema of the 1930s. In 1955 the model example of cinema was still *Chapayev* by the Vasilyev Brothers, a work which marked the beginning of Socialist realism but that had a strong dose of lyricism. It was a tightly structured epic, and the fact that I preferred Western cinema over our own Polish cinema—and certainly more than Soviet cinema—was frowned upon. The next generation was influenced much more by Italian neorealism, while personally I was utterly enthralled by *Citizen Kane*. So you can imagine the divisions and conflicts. It was almost as if we waged war against each other through the history of cinema.

Q: *Your relationship with Polish nationalism must have been problematic.*
A: Lots of filmmakers drew inspiration from nationalism for the subject matter of their films, something approved of by the regime, which meant easier access to funds and facilities. I considered this to be folkloric patriotism, though at one point it was the only way to get films authorized. In any case, these kinds of subjects never interested me and from the start I worked outside of nationalistic interests.

Q: *And you appreciated the work of the French* nouvelle vague *and the freedoms they enjoyed?*
A: That's why I came to France very early on. I spent more than a year here in 1961 but didn't get much done and went back to

Poland to make *Knife in the Water*. It was at this time—at the end of
1962—that I decided to leave Poland for good. The film had been
nominated for a Best Foreign Film Oscar which opened a few
doors for me. In France I wasn't *nouvelle vague* enough and really
didn't know what was expected of me, but in England I felt truly
free. It was like being in another world. Over there everything was
different: the handles on the windows that would slide up and
down like a guillotine, the cars they drove, the body language,
and the acting styles. I settled down very quickly and really wanted
to start making films because it was a place I didn't fully understand
and where I really felt I could do my own thing. For me it was a
virgin territory, though not in terms of tradition. Intellectually
speaking the country is very rich from that point of view. And
of course England in the 1960s was a very excitingplace, an
environment I needed to experience. I wanted to be able to meet
lots of different people. There was a cultural renaissance with
English and European artists, graphic designers, and photographers,
and also many Americans—all the filmmakers, screenwriters, and
actors who'd fled the crisis in Hollywood at the time.

Q: *All the same you used a mixture of French actors—Catherine Deneuve
and Françoise Dorléac—as well as English and American actors.
Why?*
A: I wanted to highlight the distance that exists between nations,
hence Catherine Deneuve in *Repulsion* and Françoise Dorléac in
Cul-de-sac. They weren't always at ease acting in English, and this
created something unsettling which was implicit in the films right
from the start and which I immediately picked up on. I thrive in
this kind of atmosphere—the joy of discovery and the feeling of
being deep inside my private universe. It creates a flexibility that
allows my thoughts to wander. All this was happening in the
Swinging Sixties with all these never-ending parties. It seemed as
if everything was moving around me, leading and inspiring me.
No—it's actually more that I was aspiring to the objects, language,
and rhythms around me—the whole medley. They were the happiest
years of my life, just as they were for anyone who was lucky enough
to have been caught up in it all.

Q: The Fearless Vampire Killers *seems part of this kind of cinema. It's an American film made in a studio in London with a story set in an imaginary Transylvania.*
A: It's a bit like Ionesco who was drawn toward French culture and who wrote in French, yet always brought his own ideas with him. I've always done the same, and this is what The Fearless Vampire Killers is about. The film has central European sensibilities but was filmed from an American perspective with a lot of confusion and laughter. There's also something profoundly English about it. For me, exile is about this need to travel. It's always been stimulating to me.

Q: *Out of all the exiles, who do you relate to most?*
A: Billy Wilder, without a doubt. He expresses an ironic middle-European sentiment in all his films. A purely American filmmaker would never take irony so far that it becomes absurd, but Wilder's Hollywood films are still very much the work of a European. They contain moments of a genuine "cinema of exile," something I hope my own films also have. Take the ridiculous accident that decides the outcome of the characters in Sabrina. The hero sits on some glass and cuts his backside. Wilder carries what was meant to be only a small digression as far as it'll go and then comes back to it again and again. The hero is always falling flat on his face, a trivial irony that determines the rest of the film. And it's the same kind of thing in Chinatown: no real American would ever have included the band-aid on Nicholson's nose—only a displaced European would do something like that.

Q: *Was the journey to Hollywood in the '30s and '40s the same as it was in the '70s?*
A: To tell you the truth, I never thought about it at the time. Everything in the past is history, and you can't be a proper filmmaker by concentrating solely on what's already been. It weighs you down too much. I've never really been that much of a movie buff because it all seems a bit too much like a film school exam.
   The first exiles were from an altogether other era. I encountered some of the remaining survivors at Beverly Hills soirées but preferred to keep my distance. In fact, looking back at those times today, I see that I was in a comet's tail of one era—living through the end of the Hollywood

studio system—and in the headlights of another, that of American cinema of the 1970s. It was quite strange, though there was nothing innocent about it all. Nothing that foreigners do in Hollywood is innocent, and it was at this time—caught between these two periods—when I found my footing.

Q: *In England you were caught between two worlds, in Hollywood between two eras.*
A: You could say that, yes. For example I never wanted to settle down in America, and I never lived there continuously—I always kept my house in London. What reassured me was the quality of the work Hollywood was doing, something I'd aspired to ever since my training in Poland. But Hollywood is a trap. It's so comfortable, it has such an integrating force that my way of resisting it—combined with my own European-ness and my ironic way of looking at things—was to refuse to spend much time there. I have, for instance, always been faster as a director than the American norm demands and am considered an outsider in Hollywood, though I've never really suffered because of this, except perhaps when it comes to voting at Oscar time.

Q: *You're one of those rare filmmakers who have moved back and forth between Europe and Hollywood.*
A: I like London and Paris too much to be able to detach myself totally from them. I packed my bags but still kept my house there. London in the 1970s, Paris in the 1980s—these were the two places I repeatedly left but to where I would always return. You can see it in the films I've made. After *Chinatown* I needed to make a more European film and wanted to be in France, and also do some acting, so I made *The Tenant* in Paris.

Q: *You took what you call your "irony" to Hollywood. But what did you bring back to Europe?*
A: I brought back a certain way of looking at things which evokes a sense of displacement. In *The Tenant*, for example, Paris looks like an exotic city—the Paris of a foreigner. In *Frantic* an American's gaze guides the entire film. How does an American who arrives at dawn in Roissy airport see the outskirts of Paris from his hotel? It's not the Paris

imagined by American cinema, films like *Irma la Douce* and *An American in Paris*. It's Paris seen in a very realistic way with all the tiny details, but where everything is interpreted through the lens of a different culture, through American eyes.

Q: *Tess doesn't seem to fit into this thinking. It's not about a foreigner in a realistic environment, it's more of a film that takes into account the romantic European myth with its settings and clichés. Does the mixture of actors and a culturally ambitious subject matter signal an about turn, a nostalgic desire to settle down?*

A: Maybe. I see it more as wanting to let my roots grow rather than make an about turn. But I haven't actually ever really stopped changing directions, to the point where I'm afraid of going round in circles. There's always quite a bit of time between my work, even if I do make films fairly frequently. I think this is so I have time to make these changes in direction. Above all I like to grow as a person. "Grow" is a very important word for me. I like to change scenery, to rediscover old things or move toward the new. I'm not betraying anything in doing this, I'm "growing." That's the word: I've grown whilst always doing exactly what I've wanted to do.

Q: *But again this question: what did you bring back from America to Europe?*

A: Technique. I've always liked it when a film is well made, something I got good at while I was in Hollywood. I found the best technicians in the world there, people who really know how to make films. They polish them to perfection.

Q: *We get the impression that there is a contemporary group of filmmakers that you are a part of, directors who are able to work anywhere, like a worldwide cinema show.*

A: What matters is the logical structure and action of the story being told. Naturally it has to be set somewhere, and it's this marriage of the action to a specific place that's important, something that can happen anywhere in the world. What's essential is that it's anchored in something concrete. Even in the case of fantasy film or utopian cinema you still need to create a definite and tangible culture within your invented landscape—like the costumes, the customs, and everyday objects.

Q: *In your latest film,* Bitter Moon, *you set the action on a cruise liner, a relatively neutral location.*

A: But the hero on the ship tells a story that takes place in Paris, and it's precisely the meeting of these two universes that gives the film its special qualities. You have the utopia of a cruise liner filmed realistically, and then the reality of the tale being told. Likewise, the hero played by Peter Coyote is an American—a foreigner living in Paris—a detail not in the original novel, but one that gives the story more momentum. It lends more realism to everything he sees and does. Nothing needs to be invented because he's already distanced from things.

Q: *You use the word "distance" [décalé and décalage] quite often. Is it very much a part of your cinema and, in turn, of your audiences? Maybe as if, for example, your audience were in the same position as Harrison Ford in* Frantic *who is in Paris but remains at a "distance" to the city.*

A: Of all Milos Forman's films, I like the American ones the most, and Skolimowski's English films are the ones that really touch me. My way of feeling European is effectively to be distanced, first within American films but also in relation to European cinema itself. Even my favorite European novel—Jerzy Kosinski's *The Painted Bird*—resembles this paradox, this "distance." It's written in English and is very much an American novel, but tells the story of a Jewish boy in the Ukraine during the war. So my favorite European book is actually an American one. It's rather strange that America is never really America. It's always questioning itself a little bit, while Europe dreams of being a little bit American but never quite gets there.

Blood and Emotions

MARC WEITZMANN / 1995

W: *What drew you to the idea of making a film of Ariel Dorfman's play* Death and the Maiden?

P: I've always been attracted to the kind of story where each character gives their account of the same story, like *Rashomon* and *Citizen Kane*, and I wanted to work with a story that would allow me to explore this.

W: *Why did you add a conclusion that does not appear in the play?*

P: To make the story more coherent. The play is ambiguous right up until the end, but I'd say this ambiguity is more accidental than by design. Though I like the idea of a story where you don't know who's guilty until the last minute, this works only if it fits with the theme. This wasn't the case with *Death and the Maiden* which, quite simply, was in need of a third act, otherwise I felt it would be frustrating for the audience.

W: *You even added some ambiguous episodes, for example the scene where we see Paulina talking to her husband on the balcony. Suddenly, in the background, the silhouette of Miranda appears.*

P: His hands are tied behind his back.

W: *But the impression it gives is that he's waiting for them, as if at some point he accepts the situation he finds himself in.*

P: But I think he does accept it. I tried to make the film as credible and realistic as possible. In real life prisoners don't try to escape—it only happens in the movies.

From *Première*, April 1995. Reprinted by permission. Translated by Paul Cronin and Remi Guillochon.

W: *In the film all three characters play the role of victim, accomplice, and executioner. Did you feel close to one of them in particular?*

P: I felt close to all three of them in turn, though especially to the husband Roberto. In fact I found his role the most interesting.

W: *There is something cannibalistic about the film, for example when Paulina leans on the sleeping Miranda and smells him before she hits him, or when we see a half-eaten chicken leg on the bed.*

P: I didn't think of cannibals while shooting those scenes. It was only to create a dissonant atmosphere.

W: *In the film you point towards Paulina's apparent madness. Sigourney Weaver is reminiscent of the role you played in* The Tenant.

P: Really? It wasn't done consciously, but for the film to work it was essential that Roberto doubts her.

W: *You seem to be making less disturbing films these days.*

P: I don't really think I've made *any* disturbing films. Which of my films do you think are disturbing? Perhaps *The Tenant*. What else? Maybe *Cul-de-sac.*

W: *What about* Repulsion, *where Deneuve becomes so paranoid that she starts to kill the men around her?*

P: *Repulsion?* It's not disturbing at all.

W: *What about* Tess? *And* Chinatown *is really quite strange. Does paranoid and obsessive behavior that interest you?*

P: Of course they interest me, but I'm not the only one. Don't they interest you? Words have so much weight when people ask questions like, "You like bread don't you?" Suddenly the most unimportant questions are blown out of all proportion, dangerously so. "Isn't it interesting that you like bread?" You like wine, after all. I saw you order some, but I didn't order any. You like wine, but actually I like it too.

W: *But I'd very much like you to talk about it.*

P: About wine?

w: *No, about paranoia.*

p: But I'm not paranoid! I just find it interesting. Paranoia lets you delve deeper into a character. We all have our own fears and worries, and the exploitation of such things isn't necessarily unpleasant for audiences. When I make films, I'm simply a member of the audience who cooks himself something to eat. I make films I'd like to see in the cinema. The problem is that once the meal's ready, I'm so sick that I'm not able to appreciate it.

w: *So you're telling me I'm making you talk about a film that doesn't really interest you?*

p: Yes, of course. I really don't know how anyone else manages it.

w: *Of all the films you've made, which is your favorite?*

p: I can't say there's been a film that I'm completely satisfied with. I don't think I've yet made a film which I could be truly proud of. Whenever I watch my work I'm actually ashamed of certain scenes.

w: *For example?*

p: I don't know, I don't want to talk about it. Why do you ask me things like that? [*laughs*] There are always problems with the rhythm, for example. Let's just say that some films are better made than others, like *Rosemary's Baby*. Even though it's well directed, there are still some things I don't like, especially the theme of the film. I wasn't particularly proud of doing it, but I made *Rosemary's Baby* because I needed the money. It was put together quite well, even if there are things in it that could have been better.

w: Chinatown?

p: Not bad, but it's a bit long, isn't it? It seems never-ending.

w: *According to the autobiography of the film's producer, Robert Evans, everyone thought that after the first screening in Hollywood they had a turkey on their hands.*

p: Really? My memory of the screening was being at Evans's house in the company of Charlie Bludhorn, head of Gulf and Western, the conglomerate that swallowed up Paramount. Evans was the head of the studio and had organized a screening for him. The air-conditioning was on full blast, and I was shivering when the film started, so I moved over to Bob, leaning on the console between us which had lots of buttons on it—including the air-conditioning—and said, "Can we lower it a little, I'm freezing my balls off." "Charlie has come in from New York," said Bob. "He's tired and I don't want him to fall asleep. I know it's cold, but if the room gets warm he'll nod off." I looked to my left and heard Charlie snoring. I said to Bob, "You might as well lower the air-conditioning. It won't make any difference, he's already asleep." After that they went to Santa Barbara for previews and for all I know it went pretty well, though some people complained about the violence. They felt there was too much blood. But what was there really? Some gunshots at the end, images of Faye Dunaway leaning on the steering-wheel with a hole in her head. Nothing much when compared to Sam Peckinpah's films which were fashionable at the time. That's when I understood that it's not the amount of blood split but what you do with it that matters.

W: *What about the scene when Jack Nicholson gets his nose slashed.*
P: But what is it really to cut someone's nose? It's just a nose.

W: *Why did you decide to play the nose-slasher?*
P: For fun. I enjoyed it.

W: *Are there things in* The Tenant *that you're not happy with?*
P: Yes, unfortunately. I would like to remake some of my films, or at least reedit certain scenes.

W: *Can you think of one scene in particular?*
P: The scene where I meet the beggar on my way home, for example. You know, film editing requires real stamina. There are often lots of things that might be good in themselves but upset the rhythm of a film as a whole. At one time I thought I could even cut the soliloquies from Shakespeare's plays. Without "To be or not to be" *Hamlet* is still the same play. It doesn't make any difference to the action, though sometimes you have to be careful of that way of doing thing. [*laughter*]

Ben-Hur's Riding Crop

LAURENT VACHAUD / 1995

v: Death and the Maiden *is a title that could apply equally well to several of your films.* Repulsion, Rosemary's Baby, Chinatown, *and* Tess *all come to mind.*

P: Yes, though there would have to be good reason to use it, and I wouldn't have done so here if it weren't for the dramatic device that Schubert's string quartet plays in the film.

v: Death and the Maiden *is adapted from Ariel Dorfman's play. Why did you never make the film version of Peter Schaffer's play* Amadeus *which you staged ten years ago?*

P: I would have liked to make the film version but unfortunately Saul Zaentz had bought the rights and he'd already made a deal with Milos Forman. I think I would have made a better film.

What really attracted me to *Death and the Maiden* was the character of Paulina. I've always preferred the central protagonists of my films to be female, and though I generally like female characters who are victims, Paulina is very different in this respect. Even if she's been a victim in the past, she's holding the gun now, so to speak. She reminds me of the heroine in Abel Ferrara's *Ms. 45.* There were several aspects of Dorfman's story that appealed to me, especially the question of the relativity of truth. I've always been keen on films like *Rashomon* and *Citizen Kane* which present their stories from several different viewpoints. I'd like to

From *Positif,* April 1995. Reprinted by permission of Michel Ciment. Translated by Paul Cronin and Remi Guillochon.

make a film like this one day, where the story is told by several people, each with their own version. Filming *Death and the Maiden* was quite a challenge as there are only three characters, one setting, and a very concentrated plot.

V: *You seem to like stories that take place behind closed doors.*
P: My preference for this kind of thing has its origins in my childhood, and has certainly been influenced by my time working in the theater. The first films that really had an impact on me took place in enclosed spaces—or had rather theatrical settings—for example *Hamlet* with Laurence Olivier and Carol Reed's *Odd Man Out*, one of my favorite films, superior I think to *The Third Man* where the ending is such a let-down. What really grabbed me when I saw *Odd Man Out* at the age of sixteen was the heavy atmosphere that hangs over everyone in the town.

V: *How close is the film to Dorfman's original play?*
P: I changed some of it but on the whole it's very faithful. Someone who has seen the play only once probably wouldn't even notice the changes we've made. We had to make the film more realistic in places because the play was too contrived and conventional. For example in the play, when Paulina hits Miranda, he's out cold for too long. I've been hit in the head quite badly on occasion so I know that fainting is never very authentic in films. These are the kinds of details that have been changed. But we focused our real work on the structure because the play has no real third act. There's no feeling of any resolution to the story despite that fact that it was written as a whodunnit in which the suspense revolves around the search for a culprit. I found this quite frustrating, so we added a third act. Miranda's final confession isn't in the original.

V: *The film has an unusually well-defined structure. It begins with Paulina and her husband in a concert hall listening to Schubert's quartet. Paulina is clearly not feeling well, and then the flashback about the story with the doctor begins. When Miranda confesses at the end, we move back to Paulina and her husband in the concert hall to discover that Miranda is sitting near them with his family. Was this your idea?*
P: Yes. The play ended with a theatrical device whereby a mirror is lowered in front of the audience that is reflected in it. Everyone can see

there are three empty seats. Then Paulina, her husband and Miranda come and sit down.

Dorfman's play is about reconciliation. He wants to suggest that after the fall of a dictatorship, victims will occasionally come face to face with their torturers in the street. From now on, these people will be crossing each other's paths in everyday life.

v: *A film with no deaths is a novelty for you. When you made* Chinatown *you argued with Robert Towne to have the Faye Dunaway character murdered. In* Frantic, *Emmanuelle Seigner is killed, and in* Bitter Moon, *the Benton couple commit suicide. But in* Death and the Maiden, *everyone survives.*

p: Yes, but it's much worse in *Death and the Maiden.* It's important for every story to have the most effective possible ending. Not every author of great literature wants his readers to feel completely comfortable at the end of the story, and I've done the same here. If Paulina had exacted her revenge on Miranda it would have been a much weaker ending. The audience would have nothing to think about and would have forgotten the film immediately after leaving the cinema. I like to make audiences question what they've seen and think about things, in this case justice.

It's true that I like unhappy endings because to me they're more truthful. With *Bitter Moon,* the last chapter of Pascal Bruckner's book seemed out of joint with the rest of the novel. He came up with a whole load of complex scheming to explain the hero's confession, but I felt it was more logical that the film ended with the Benton couple committing suicide.

v: *How did you come to work with the novelist Rafael Iglesias on the script? He also wrote* Fearless *for Peter Weir.*

p: *Death and the Maiden* was a Warner Bros. project because they had the rights to the play, and I developed the project for them when Peter Weir's film was being shot. Warner Bros. recommended Rafael Iglesias to me. I didn't know him but our collaboration worked out very well. He's quick and clever, and the fact that he's a novelist means he has a good working knowledge of his craft.

v: *How did you first hear about the play?*

p: I never saw it on stage though I did read the manuscript when the play was on in London at the Royal Court. It had a successful run there before it moved to the West End. The script has been around a lot because it's so commercial. I didn't know the actors in the London production, but when it was staged on Broadway by Mike Nichols, Glenn Close and Richard Dreyfuss played Paulina and her husband, and Gene Hackman played Miranda.

v: *How did Sigourney Weaver come to play Paulina in the film?*

p: It's funny how that came about. Her agent contacted us to let us know she was interested in the part. We thought that if such a well-known actress was willing to join such a difficult project then we'd better make the most of it. She's one of the few American actresses you can count on at the box-office, and with Sigourney signed to a film it's easier to raise money. On top of that, she appeared just when Warner Bros. were wondering if there was any real commercial potential in the project. Most distributors look the other way when you pitch them a story about human rights that takes place in a single location with three actors, but Sigourney's involvement won them over.

v: *You gave the part of the torturer to Ben Kingsley. He'd just done* Schindler's List *where he played a good Samaritan. Was this intentionally ironic?*

p: Absolutely not. I didn't even consider it. I just wanted someone who didn't look like a torturer for the part.

v: *What about Stuart Wilson?*

p: I didn't know him at all. The role of the husband was the most difficult to cast, and I came across Stuart by chance. I had seen him in Martin Scorsese's *The Age of Innocence* and *Lethal Weapon 3*, where he played a baddy.

v: *In several of your films there are American and British actors, and* Death and the Maiden *is no exception. Sigourney Weaver is American, and Ben Kingsley and Stuart Wilson are English.*

p: On the whole I prefer to work with English actors. There are so many talented and professional actors in England who are a real gold

mine for directors. Generally speaking, American actors don't have
the same technique, and because of this sometimes it can be
interesting to cast them opposite English actors. They're more into
method acting and don't have as much theatrical experience.
They've learnt their craft at acting schools or on television and are
less patient than English actors, many of whom have spent the
early part of their careers in repertory theater. But American actors
are still easier to work with than the French because they always
know their lines.

V: Death and the Maiden *deals with the traumas of your own life
for the first time, like living under a dictatorship and being accused
of rape.*
P: I knew what I was talking about when I made this film. I was
able to use my own experiences and put myself in the shoes of these
characters. But I don't make any connection between this story and
my own life. It's certainly not why I made the film.

V: *You once said what drew you to* Amadeus *was that you could understand the two viewpoints: Mozart's and Salieri's. Have you tried to identify
with all three characters with this film?*
P: I would find it very difficult to identify with Miranda, but
I did try to make him as humane as possible by trying to examine
his motives and discover what lay behind his behavior. I wanted
him to articulate these things and had to show him as objectively
as possible.

That's how I directed Ben Kingsley. Without telling the other two
actors, I asked him to play Miranda as if he were totally innocent.
I wanted the audience to question his apparent guilt from the start,
which from a philosophical point of view made for a more interesting
dynamic between the three of them. You could well imagine an
innocent man constructing a convincing confession in order to
save his neck. You told me I've been accused of rape, but this isn't
quite true. I've actually been found guilty of illegal sexual acts,
in other words sex with a minor. At the time it was called
"statutory rape," though the newspapers chose to use only the
word "rape."

v: *Rape is something that has featured quite often in your films, for exam-*
ple Tess *and* Chinatown, *where the father is raping his daughter at the same*
time as city of Los Angeles is being taken advantage of.
P: Maybe, but it's not something I'm conscious of. Even if there are
female characters in my films who are victims, I don't especially like
rape stories. *Chinatown* was written by Robert Towne, so it wasn't my
idea to write this kind of story.

v: *After the commercial failure of* The Tenant *you decided to concentrate on*
films like Pirates *and* Frantic. *Back then you said something like, "Entertain-*
ment comes first."
P: Yes, I'd had it up to here with arty and *auteur*-driven films. Sometimes
you just want to have fun when making a film. Don't forget that for a
director, a film represents a whole year of his life, sometimes even
more, so it's important to choose what kind of atmosphere you want to
immerse yourself in, as it's bound to influence your state of mind. I
remember it was pretty horrible when I acted in Guiseppe Tornatore's *A*
Pure Formality. The set was cold and dank, and there were candles and
water strewn all over the floor. It was a very depressing atmosphere. The
only plus was Gérard Depardieu who cheered me up no end. He has a
great sense of humor and boundless energy. I think that even for
Tornatore it must have been difficult to work there day in, day out.

v: *Is the reason you prefer to do stories with fewer characters because you*
find shooting period films like Tess *and* Pirates *so exhausting?*
P: Yes, but now I feel ready to tackle something more wide ranging
and epic. Generally speaking, I always react against the film I've just
done. For the next film I want to do something completely different.

v: *There are lots of monologues in* Death and the Maiden, *like Ben*
Kingsley's confession.
P: I wanted to do it like that, rather than a series of dialogues.

v: *You filmed the confession in close-up without any cuts. This seems a*
bold choice in view of most contemporary cinema which has speeded up
because of the influence of trailers and television.
P: I'm fortunate to be able to do things my way. There aren't many
close-ups in my films and this is why everybody noticed that scene.

V: *Do you have everything precisely planned in your head when you shoot a film?*

P: No. I use storyboards only for sequences that involve special effects or a lot of detail, like in *Pirates*. Otherwise I don't like storyboarding because it's too limiting. It's like having an expert couturier make a suit for you and then trying to find someone to fit into it. I prefer to work with the actors from the beginning. I observe what they do during rehearsals and only afterwards make decisions about how to edit the scene. Telling them what to do from the start kills their spontaneity and creativity. I like to work with talented actors because I expect them to bring something to their work. The way they move and talk is far more natural and interesting than anything I could ask of them, even if I am quite good at inventing things.

V: *Did the actors enjoy filming in such an enclosed environment?*

P: We were afraid that by the end of the third week we'd all be at each other's throats suffering from cabin fever, but it didn't happen. A month before the end of the shoot we decided to go to Spain for a week to take a break and shoot all the exteriors. But even though it was a pleasant week, we didn't really need it. The set where the film was shot was so well built, artistically and practically speaking. You know how much I enjoy shooting in a studio—it's a working environment where I feel truly comfortable. Those directors who don't like studios obviously don't know how to use them properly. They think filming there will mean everything will look more artificial than if they'd been on location, but that's just nonsense. Of course I don't have anything against shooting on location, but you have to agree that the final results are usually not as good as what's possible in a studio. On location everything is often adversely affected by what's going on around you, and sometimes you just aren't able to get certain shots you want. You can see the scene from only one angle—the one dictated by the lay-out of the location itself.

I'm the product of a film school, so how could I ever approve of amateurism? With *Frantic*, for example, it was easier for me to show what a Parisian hotel looks like by shooting in a studio than in a real hotel. I could never have achieved such a natural effect in a real hotel bedroom because I wouldn't have been able to place the huge lights in the right places to create the glow of dawn I wanted. And where would the crew have been if we'd shot in a real hotel? In the corridor? It just doesn't make sense.

V: *Which scenes in* Death and the Maiden *were the most difficult to shoot?*
P: Primarily the scene on the verandah when Pauline is telling her husband about what happened to her. I wanted to shoot it on three levels: Paulina, her husband, and—in the background behind the window pane—Miranda pacing up and down inside the house. I found it quite tricky because originally I had a completely different idea. I'd thought that at this moment in the film it would be better to ease the tension and lighten things up. That's why I had Sigourney and Stuart stand in front of this landscape of the sky and the sea. I shot the scene that way but during editing immediately realized it didn't work and that I should have chosen the reverse shot instead, which put Sigourney and Stuart in front of the window of the house. That's what we filmed after coming back from Spain.

V: *Even with material as static as a stage play, you're always trying to give the audience more than one way of looking at the images.*
P: Yes, but this is a very fundamental idea, don't you think? If I hadn't done this—if I'd simply pointed lights at the actors and made them talk like they do in French films—you wouldn't be here interviewing me now.

V: *What sort of relationship do you have with critics?*
P: There seem to be fewer and fewer people who really know how to watch films. Most critics form an opinion about a film director that never changes, which makes me sometimes wonder if they aren't blind. And there's trick among critics that I find amusing. Have you seen [the Paris listings magazine] *Pariscope*? If you went along with the critics, [Gérard Corbiau's 1994 film] *Farinelli*—which has three stars—is better than *Dr. Strangelove*, with only two. Or how about [Jacques Audiard's 1994 film] *Regard les hommes tomber* which apparently is as good as *Citizen Kane* or *Jour de fête*. Everybody seems to have lost their bearings. I get the feeling that many critics resent film directors who make only genre films or who like to tell real stories. But I don't really know what's behind it all.

v: *You still find it important to start with, "Once upon a time . . . ,"*
something that's apparent in films like Bitter Moon *and to a certain extent*
Death and the Maiden, *where you show one character telling a story to a*
spellbound listener.
p: More than anything I just want to tell a good story. That's what
drives me. When I was at film school we were all so eager to be story-
tellers and were worried we might make films where nothing happened,
where things were just like everyday life. This just wasn't modern
enough for us. To me, modernity is about showing something that's
dramatically compelling. I'm also fond of turning stereotypes on their
head.

v: *There are shots in* Bitter Moon *that some audiences felt were utterly*
devoid of irony, for example the scene where Peter Coyote kisses Emmanuelle
Seigner for the first time in front of a blazing fire—something we've seen in
countless love scenes.
p: Yes, but the whole film is full of these kinds of things simply
because I love cinema. First and foremost, I like to put my favorite
images from other films into my own work. Directors always make the
same film over and over again, and for some of them their knowledge
of life in general seems to be drawn exclusively from what they've seen
at the cinema.

Harrison Ford once told me an amusing story about Steven Spielberg.
He was in Sri Lanka with Spielberg filming the second Indiana Jones film.
There was a scene where he had to ride an elephant and they were
about to roll the camera when Spielberg insisted that the boy who was
leading the elephant get rid of his riding crop because, according to
Spielberg, it wasn't a real one. "How do you know?" asked Harrison. "I
know because I've seen a real one, and it doesn't look like that," said
Spielberg. "Where did you see a real riding crop?" asked Harrison. "I can't
remember," says Spielberg. The next day Spielberg goes up to Harrison
and says, "You know where I've seen a riding crop? It was in *Ben-Hur.*"

v: *You've had a much more varied and full life than Spielberg but have*
refused to make use of these experiences for your films.
p: I've had plenty of life experience, yes. I've traveled, in particular to
Tibet when I went trekking. But in spite of all that, when I make a film

or work on a script, I find that everything I have to contribute comes from cinema itself. My experiences have helped me make events more plausible and realistic, but they've never served as the starting point for the stories I tell. I wrote my autobiography to explain this, and that's all there is to it. I should add that I tend to mistrust this notion of linking a filmmaker's life with his work.

v: *But when you made* Bitter Moon *weren't you toying with this idea? You cast your wife in this tale of sadomasochism where the hero is a rootless artist full of unbridled sexuality. Some of the dialogue Peter Coyote speaks is even taken word for word from your autobiography, which led some critics to assume that you were identifying yourself with this character.*

P: Maybe I'm a little naïve, but I didn't set to provoke anyone when I made *Bitter Moon*. The story seems so over the top. How could it have anything to do with my own life? It's true some of the details were suggested by what my wife had said to me and by what I've seen myself, but these are the kind of building blocks that all artists use. When Mimi stands up naked and looks at the rising sun in *Bitter Moon*, it's true that Peter Coyote reads the description of my first wife Basia from my autobiography. But so what? This doesn't mean the film has anything inherently to do with my life. In fact, I'm the opposite of Peter Coyote's character. I'm rational and organized, not wild and shambolic. People who know me can testify to this.

v: *Why did you never adapt Jerzy Kosinski's book* The Painted Bird, *the story of a young Jewish boy sheltered by Polish peasants during the Second World War? It's a very similar story to what you went through yourself.*

P: What really bothered me was having the Ukranian peasants and the little boy speaking English. As I don't see the film being shot in Polish, I've never given much thought to the idea.

v: *And yet with* Schindler's List, *Spielberg has shown that a film about these events can make sense in English.*

P: That film challenged some of my preconceptions. In fact, it helped me with *Death and the Maiden* because the story takes place in a Latin American country and I had to do it in English. Several years ago Spielberg suggested I make *Schindler's List* but I refused after considering this language problem. But this wasn't the main reason why I said no to him. The story was too similar to my own life and I just felt I couldn't make a good film about these kinds of things. I certainly wouldn't have done as good a job as Spielberg because I couldn't have been as objective as he was. His approach was akin to Dickens's when he wrote about the French Revolution in *A Tale of Two Cities*.

v: *What are you working on at the moment?*

P: I'm in that strange time in between films. I spoke about this with Stanley Kubrick who asked me if I found this as difficult as he did. I do find it tough, but only because I have several projects to chose from. One is an adaptation of Bulgakov's *The Master and the Margarita*, another is *Les Misérables*, one is a parody of *Cendrillon*. I'd also like to make a film in Poland.

Filmmaking Is a Roulette Game

JULIAN HANICH/1999

H: *What does this retrospective at the Munich Film Festival mean to you?*
P: I'm confused. On the one hand they organize a retrospective for me. On the other hand I can't stand it when people look at my first attempts at filmmaking done when I was still at film school. I want to hide under the seat when I see them.

H: *As well as making films, you have acted and directed in the theater.*
P: Theater is like therapy after a movie. Making films always takes up so much time. When I started, directors would make one film a year. Today it's only every three years. With theater everything happens in a few months and the obstacles aren't so big, which means more freedom. Also the people you deal with are much more cultivated and less business-like. The movie business has become a roulette game: most films lose money, a few make a fortune, and the main concern today is, "How do I make big bucks?"

H: *But there are always new attempts to break out of this game, like the Dogme films from Denmark.*
P: This is what every filmmaker who wants to be original has to struggle with, and it's something that's always existed. But you couldn't call it a general tendency. These people are part of the avant-garde—though with regard only to their ideas and not in the way they execute them.

From *Der Tagesspiegel*, 2 July 1999. Reprinted by permission. Translated by Moritz Gimbel and Paul Cronin.

[Thomas Vinterberg's 1998 Dogme feature] *The Celebration,* for example, had fantastic actors and an exciting story. But why torture your audience with a shaking camera? You don't know if the cameraman is holding the camera with his left hand and masturbating with his right. Time and again one of these films makes it at a festival, the press writes about it and it's laden with awards. But how many people actually like it? Thank God there are festivals where every now and then it's possible to see interesting films from Africa or Asia, work that never makes it into distribution because today everything's a question of money.

H: *Can you judge a film by the number of viewers it attracts?*
P: We make films so people see them. Can you imagine a director who watches his movies alone? Film is a form of expression, and to express something means to share it with others. The greatest actor is nothing in an empty theater.

H: *Where do you see the most important aesthetic tendencies in cinema today?*
P: Aesthetic is not quite the right word. Judged aesthetically, *Life Is Beautiful* is a very bad film—neither the photography nor the leading actress is very good. But it's still fantastic, one of the most interesting films in recent years, because it's entertaining and philosophical at the same time. Is it possible to talk of aesthetics in this context?

H: *George Lucas has predicated that the cinema of the future will be defined entirely by digital technology.*
P: That's a natural evolution and I just hope it happens quickly. Think about how films are made today: we still have frames on a strip of film running in front of a lens in this archaic way. It's something out of the nineteenth century! At the same time there's a digital way to capture and reproduce images, and it's affordable for everyone. We filmmakers really are stuck in the past.

Depth Isn't Important to Me

RÜDIGER STURM / 1999

S: *You used to be constantly surrounded by paparazzi. What happened to them?*
P: They vanished a long time ago.

S: *Do you miss them?*
P: How would you feel being constantly harassed? Today I can live as a normal human being.

S: *Before there didn't seem to be any real difference between your public and private lives.*
P: But that wasn't my fault. Everything started with the Sharon Tate tragedy which happened shortly after the success of *Rosemary's Baby*. The film was about witchcraft and then there was this unfortunate murder that wasn't solved for a long time. So what do the media do when they run out of ideas? They speculate. They're awfully creative.

S: *You have returned to the theme of occultism with* The Ninth Gate. *Are you afraid of being mocked again?*
P: I don't take those kind of accusations seriously. I'm able to do films like this because I'm not religious. And anyway, the story is completely different from *Rosemary's Baby*.

From *Die Woche*, 6 August 1999. Reprinted by permission of Rüdiger Sturm. Translated by Tamara Kraljic and Paul Cronin.

S: *Were you focused during production?*
P: I sure was. I think I take more pleasure now in filmmaking than I ever have. But not for the reason that maybe you're thinking of.

S: *Which is?*
P: That it's this whole "art" cinema thing and the philosophical depth of filmmaking that interest me. That's not important to me at all. I simply like to play with the camera, the lights, the actors. To me, filmmaking is what a train set is to a child.

S: *But you do have a reputation of being quite unforgiving with your toys. Robert Evans, who produced* Rosemary's Baby *and* Chinatown, *called you an "autocrat."*
P: There's no democracy on a film set. The director has a vision of a film that he has to get into the heads of everyone involved.

S: *Is this why you pulled Faye Dunaway's hair when making* Chinatown?
P: The hair in question was reflecting the light and would have completely ruined the shot. Instead of being thankful, she wanted me fired.

S: *John Travolta didn't let it get to that. A few days before starting work on* The Double, *he quit.*
P: That was two years ago but I still haven't forgiven him. So many people had put so much effort into that project when all of a sudden everything fell apart. Pierre Guffroy, my longtime production designer, cried when we tore down the set.

S: *Were there rational grounds for the cancellation of the film?*
P: Travolta claimed I'd changed the script without him agreeing. Besides the fact that it was within my rights to do so, the whole thing was a joke. On the other hand, looking back, it was probably a good thing in the end because of all the special effects needed. It required a lot of patience and I don't think Travolta would have been up to it.

S: *Despite this, do you still want to work with big movie stars?*
P: Stars are, after all, an audience attraction, though that doesn't make their wages any less obscene. How can Travolta—who gets $20 million—risk such silly behavior? But there are plenty of

counterexamples, like Sigourney Weaver who asked for a third of her usual fee for *Death and the Maiden,* and Johnny Depp who was very disciplined when we made *The Ninth Gate.*

S: *You aren't exactly cheap yourself. You have a reputation of always going over budget.*
P: If you want a stack of film reels which reflect your vision, you have to use everything in your power. And with my last three films I didn't go over budget.

S: *But those films didn't bring in much money either.*
P: Nowadays the studios do nothing but count their dollars. It used to be possible for a great film to be made without it being a huge success, and despite this the studios were proud of it all the same. This just doesn't happen anymore, which is why there are fewer and fewer interesting films being made.

S: *So you are less enthusiastic today about filmmaking?*
P: As far as the business side goes, yes. The managers who run the studios have to justify their existence somehow, so they organize endless "creativity meetings." It's absolutely impossible that a mass of people like that could ever come up with a good idea. Films just can't be made in committees.

S: *Would you return to Hollywood?*
P: Only for a visit. I am, and always will remain, European. Back in the seventies, when I was working over there, I would fly back to my house in London as soon as filming was done.

S: *The atmosphere of your films is somewhat European—quite morbid and sarcastic. Why are there so few happy endings to your films?*
P: Take *Chinatown* for example. The author wanted Faye Dunaway to shoot the bad guy at the end but I was against it. The bad guy couldn't be punished, otherwise nothing would have made sense. What you want is the audience to walk out of the cinema and think about the film afterward, right? That's why you can't show a few injustices and then make everything okay at the end. You shouldn't satisfy the audience's expectations at every stage.

S: *That's not exactly a formula for success.*

P: Let's assume that in the future there are interactive cinemas where the audience can change the direction a story by pressing a button. We get to the famous "boy meets girl" scene. The two want to marry but have to get permission from their parents. If it were up to the audience to decide yes or no, most of them would want them to get married and that would be end of the story.

S: *So is the audience stupid?*

P: It's not stupid, it's just always guided by its feelings. The fact that *Titanic* ended the way it did, without any protest from the public, is one of James Cameron's greatest achievements. How could it have been otherwise? Both heroes surviving the shipwreck and living happily ever after in Pasadena?

S: *Actually, not a bad ending in the real world.*

P: Assuming you live in Paris, not Pasadena.

S: *Which reality do you prefer? The one as head of a family or that of a filmmaker?*

P: Let me put it this way: both my children—my daughter is almost seven, my son is one and half—are my best productions so far.

S: *What are your plans for the future?*

P: Ask me something easier. The older I get, the harder I find it to decide what I should do next. As a young man I was much more innocent. Life seemed endless and I simply said, "Okay: I'm doing this film. Period." Time has taught me that I have to assume all the responsibilities when I embark on one of these adventures, and today I ask myself, "Do I really have the perseverance? Can I handle everything getting on my nerves?"

S: *The director as martyr?*

P: I know it sounds pretentious, but it's not. Making films is a battle, and sometimes you get tired of fighting.

S: *Do you always have to win?*

P: I simply want to produce good work, and that's why I have to think I'm the best. Of course this isn't easy because it's not necessarily true. But you won't win if you think you're a looser.

What Does Evil Mean to You, Mr. Polanski?

RALPH GEISENHANSLÜKE / 1999

G: *Pleased to meet you, hope you guess my name.*
P: What's that supposed to mean?

G: *It's from the Rolling Stones song "Sympathy for the Devil." At the moment, a lot of films are about the Devil—including your own,* The Ninth Gate. *A millennium theme?*
P: I don't know about these other films. For me, the millennium is simply a date like any other. If anything, it demonstrates our dependency on the decimal system, nothing more.

G: *You've faced "evil," let's call it, many times in your life.*
P: Evil and the Devil are two separate things. The Devil is how humans often like to imagine evil, with horns and a tail. Evil is part of our personality.

G: *How would you define your relationship to "evil"? It seems to be a central theme of your films.*
P: I don't have a relationship to evil. I've never believed in occultism or the Devil, and I'm not at all religious. I'd rather read science books than something about occultism. When it comes to cinema, evil is simply a form of entertainment to me.

From *Der Tagesspiegel*, 15 December 1999. Reprinted by permission. Translated by Moritz Gimbel and Paul Cronin.

G: *In* The Ninth Gate *a woman takes the male protagonist to hell.*
P: Women are usually the victims in my films. This time it's the male protagonist, but he's not the nicest human being on earth, as you can see. You could speculate how this relates to my other films, but I don't think it's terribly interesting. It could just be a coincidence. I was interested in the novel on which the film is based—its atmosphere, its humor, its suspense—the material for the film, in other words. The theme of evil itself mattered even less to me.

G: *Nevertheless, it's an unusual portrait of a woman, don't you think? A woman who appears to be an angel at first but then leads the man into hell.*
P: The Devil can take any form, so they say. If he's going to have a good job, there's no point in him coming across as ugly.

G: *He is often portrayed as a very wealthy man, a Wall Street broker, for example.*
P: Really? Well, if he masters all the tricks described in the old stories, he shouldn't have a problem providing for himself.

G: *How do you explain the obsession with demonic themes in current films?*
P: It sells.

G: *It could also be that a lot of people are afraid of the future and that films speak to that fear.*
P: Well, let's put it this way: the world isn't getting any better, which is quite alienating. Scientific progress seems to amplify rather than lessen our problems. Inventions proliferate, the economy booms, but people suffer ever more.

G: *Because less people are able to participate in that progress?*
P: I think there are simply too many people. Progress can't keep up with the growing population, although we like to believe otherwise. [*Polanski stands up, fanning air into his face. The hotel room is very hot.*] Damn! There must be a switch to regulate the heating in here. My nose is totally clogged.

G: *True. It's hot as hell in here. Why don't we just open a window?*
P: Exactly! The traditional way.

G: *In your autobiography you write that you went to the cinema every day during your childhood in Krakow.*
P: Maybe not seven days a week, but almost.

G: *Did cinema offer a parallel world to you, a refuge for a Jewish kid who had to hide and grow up without parents?*
P: Yes, certainly during the German occupation, although I didn't realize it at the time. Afterwards it was simply a dream world. Even as a young boy all I wanted was to go to the cinema, and my sister would take me. Everything that had to do with the projection of film was magic to me.

G: *How do you feel about the digitalization of that magic?*
P: The more, the better.

G: *But you still use old-fashioned celluloid.*
P: Just like every other director. But I benefit greatly from digital effects and manipulation to improve what I shoot on film. It's inventions like this that help artists to express their ideas better. Some of my films would be much improved with digital effects, for example *Repulsion* with the hands coming out of the wall. With today's technology I could make the scene as surreal as I wanted to, but back then everything had to be built out of latex, plastic, and other rubbish, and we still didn't get the desired effect. The first period of my work was particularly frustrating when I was strongly influenced by Surrealism. Today's digital technology allows you to create really surreal images, just like Dali or De Chirico imagined them.

G: *Are you tempted to reshoot* Repulsion *with digital technology?*
P: God no! I would never reshoot any of my films. I'm creative enough not to dig up old stuff. The only thing I ever did twice was *The Fearless Vampire Killers* when it was turned into a musical in Vienna.

G: *You constantly go back to the theater and the opera.*

P: Yes. I try as often as possible to return to the theater between my films, though it's not always easy to unite the two disciplines. Theater has a fixed schedule while film is very different. Usually the starting date gets moved back, and don't even mention the missed deadlines. But sometimes it's possible to connect the two worlds. I recently staged *Amadeus* in Italy, and I'm sure I'll be up for another play after my next film.

G: *Your last film,* Death and the Maiden, *is already five years old. Do you have any new projects?*

P: I have ideas, but nothing is decided or signed yet.

G: *Is there an author whose work you would particularly like to stage?*

P: A really good play is always exciting, something that sticks out from the many written every year. Apart from that I love Shakespeare. He's the greatest master of all, one of my first loves. I've never had the chance to stage a Shakespeare play. I first saw *Hamlet* as a teenager, and many times since. That play is one of the reasons why I make films—it really seduced me. If I had the chance I'd stage *Macbeth* for the theater. Sure, I made a film out of it years ago, but it wasn't very fashionable to film Shakespeare at the time. There's been a recent wave of films based on his plays. So, going back to the Devil, he's not the only trend to be found at the end of the millennium. Shakespeare is also back.

Roman Polanski

CHARLIE ROSE / 2000

R: *In your heart, in your soul . . .*
P: Heart or soul?

R: *Either. Both. Are you French, Polish, something else?*
P: In my soul, I'm French. In my heart, I'm Polish, I think.

R: *Why is that?*
P: Because the heart is somehow connected with sentiment more than the soul, I would say. And since I grew up in Poland, my childhood—my youth, my schooling, film school, above all—is Polish, and so naturally my heart goes to Poland. France was always something I aspired to when we were hermetically locked in by communism in Poland. We all dreamt of going west to various places. For me it was France. I loved French movies. I loved Paris because I heard about it from my parents, you know? It was something that I always imagined, and I wanted my imagination to become reality. So my first steps were towards Paris.

R: *You went back to Krakow two days ago. What was it like for you?*
P: Oh, it was fantastic. But each time I go there I'm moved. It's a question of nostalgia. On literally every corner there's a building that reminds me of something.

R: *It would seem to me it would remind you of everything because that's where you were with your parents.*
P: Yes. That's where I lived in the ghetto. That's where I escaped from the ghetto. That's where I went to school. That's where I had my first success as a child actor. And that's where I suffered and where I had my joys of growing up. So obviously my heart's there, as I told you.

R: *Tell me about your mother.*
P: Well, my mother was taken to Auschwitz very early, in one of the first raids on the ghetto, and that was it. I never heard from her again. I was hoping for her to return. My father returned after the war, but my mother didn't.

R: *What happened to you?*
P: I lived in the country with Polish peasants in a very primitive cottage. It was virtually medieval, but the people were very good.

R: *They saved your life?*
P: They saved my life. Yes, absolutely.

R: *Did you understand what had happened to your mother?*
P: What do you mean, did I understand?

R: *When she didn't come back, did they say that she had been gassed?*
P: Yes, this I learned later from people who knew her, who were more or less in the same transport. At the beginning I didn't know what happened to my friends, and then when I was staying with an uncle, people were returning from concentration camps and labor camps. A note arrived from my father. I knew he was alive, and he returned. And then I was told that my mother was not coming back, that she was dead. So I learned about her death about two or three months after the war.

R: *How old were you?*
P: I was just twelve.

R: *I know you're not a psychologist or a psychiatrist. But what does that do, and how do you think that might be reflected—*
P: I can't answer this question. Kids accept life as it is because they don't know anything else. They can't relate to any other lives, you know? So now, when I have children, I relive it in a strange way because very often I think of myself and of my parents. I can somehow imagine them in the same situation and imagine myself in my father's skin during those times. I tell you, the hardships I went through seemed quite normal to me. What was painful was the separation from my parents. That really hurt the most, more than anything else—more than the hunger, than the cold or whatever.

R: *Not to have your parents with you.*
P: Yes, knowing they had been taken. I remember one day, playing in the fields, in the snow, when I saw a man walking towards us. For some reason I thought it was my father. He was coming closer and closer, and finally he was close enough for me to realize that it was just a peasant walking.

R: *When did you say, "I want to be in the movies. I want to be an actor or a director."*
P: I knew I wanted to make movies. I knew I wanted to be a part of it. I knew I wanted to create this because it was fantasy. It was very early on. I mean, literally as a child. The projection of film was something magical in itself. You see, I went to school only for a few weeks because the war started and there were no more schools for Jews. But in the school I remember they had a machine that could project pages from books. It had a mirror and a lens in front on the screen. It was fascinating, and I was interested in how it worked and was always trying to build projectors. This was my hobby, even when I was in the countryside.

R: *Can you tell me just how all of this shaped you, this experience and Krakow.*
P: This I can't tell you. I can tell you only the episodes of my life, of those times.

R: *You can't look back and say, "There is a direct connection between that, losing my mother, experiencing this sense of fear," and all that you just described, and knowing how it's manifest in the man you are?*
P: Well, don't you agree that whatever we experience has a result on our activity, on our passions, loves, manias? So obviously it must have, but to what extent I am unable to tell you. It's work for a psychiatrist.

R: *I know, but you're an insightful man. You think about these kinds of things, don't you?*
P: Never.

R: *Never?*
P: Absolutely never. I'm not even interested in it.

R: *You're not? You're not interested in what shapes a life?*
P: I'm interested in the world around me and my own shape, you know?

R: *It's been said that Faye Dunaway's character in* Chinatown *was in some way an image of your mother.*
P: Well, the film was about that era, and I remember how my mother made herself up and what was fashionable. I told Faye how I wanted her to look, and I remember that the Cupid bow was very fashionable. I remember doing her make-up exactly. I remember that it was fashionable to pluck the eyebrows and then draw the line. We made tests and Faye was delighted with it. But there's no need to look for some kind of deep meaning in it. It was simply that the film takes place in the late 1930s and I remember my mother at that time. Obviously I had some knowledge of what a woman should look like, but there is no association between the character and my mother.

R: *If someone said, for example, that Roman has loved women so much because he lost his mother, what would you say?*
P: There are other people who didn't lose mothers, like Warren Beatty for example, who loved women as much as I did. So how do you answer this one? It's because he didn't lose his mother.

R: *How did you get to Paris?*

P: It was much later. In those times you couldn't even dream of leaving Poland. It was like the Wall in Germany. No one was allowed a passport, no one was allowed to leave. I had my sister who went from Auschwitz back to Paris. You know, Paris was really her place. She lived there before. She was older than me. She got married after the war and I learned that she was alive living in Paris. We corresponded and she invited me to come. Then great changes happened in Poland and I finally got my passport. That was my first visit to this town and it was fabulous. You cannot imagine what it means for someone who lived in that gray, drab, communist reality to visit a Western city. Paris above all. But I was still at the film school, so I returned.

R: *At the Lodz film school you had a chance to make a movie. A short, right?*

P: Well, I did my first short films at the school. I always wanted to be a director. When I was in the theater I wanted to be a director, but the film school was such an exclusive institution that I wouldn't even have dreamt of being accepted there, so I thought about studying acting. However, I wasn't accepted in any acting schools and when I spoke to the dean of the film school he said, "Why don't you try the film school?" I said, "What chances do I have?" He said, "You won't know what chance you have if you don't try." So I tried and I got in the film school. It was one of the most fantastic days of my life when I read my name on the list. And that's how it all started.

R: *Let me just talk about the movies you've made. You moved to Paris permanently what, 1960, 1961?*

P: Yes. I moved to Paris permanently after my first feature film, *Knife in the Water*. I went back to Poland to do this film. It was very badly received by the government because of its content, lukewarmly by the press, and pretty well by the public. First it went to the Venice film festival and won the critic's prize there. Then was shown at the New York Film Festival and was on the cover of *Time* magazine. Then it was nominated for the Academy Award.

R: Knife in the Water *was on the cover of* Time *magazine?*
P: Yes, it was on the cover. It said, "Lovers in Polish Film." It's a big close-up of two characters, the girl and the boy, kissing on the yacht.

R: *Suggesting change in Poland or something?*
P: Suggesting that there are also films in Poland.

R: *But it was poorly received in Poland by the government?*
P: Yes. As a matter of fact, Gomulka, who was then prime minister of Poland, threw an ashtray at the television.

R: *Then* Repulsion *came along.*
P: An American producer of Polish origin, Gene Gutowski, suggested I come to London and make a film there, and he introduced me to several production companies. One of them was run by distributors and producers who needed respectability because they made almost skin flicks. Here was this young director, acclaimed by the press and critics, so they were willing to finance me. I needed to write something quickly that would be up their alley. With Gérard Brach, my friend with whom I wrote many scripts here in France that have never seen the light of a projector, I wrote the treatment of *Repulsion*, and they liked it.

R: *Was it easy to get Catherine Deneuve?*
P: Oh, it was very easy to get Catherine Deneuve because she knew me and I was appreciated as a young film director with a future. Catherine liked the role and she came to do it. She was a beginner herself.

R: *What do you think of her as an actress?*
P: Well, she's sometimes great. I think she's better with age. I like her performance in *Repulsion*. I think it was a very good experience for both of us. She was very receptive to my direction. It was like dancing a tango with her, truly.

R: *She's following your lead?*
P: She was following my lead, yes.

R: *And then* Rosemary's Baby.

P: No, after that came *Cul-de-sac*. And then came *The Fearless Vampire Killers*, and then came *Rosemary's Baby*.

R: *But* Rosemary's Baby *really put you on the map.*

P: Yes, indeed, because it was my first studio picture. And it was Mia, with whom it was another tango. Mia was fantastic to work with. She was really great because she's a talented actress and she loved the role and the film. She was very flexible. She would listen to me, as a director, and follow my instructions. What more can I tell you?

R: *You were about how old at this time?*

P: I was twenty-seven when I did my first feature, *Knife in the Water*. So, that must have been four or five years later.

R: *You were in Rome when the Manson murder took place?*

P: No, I was in London actually.

R: *You've talked about this before, and I don't want to go into it at length. But—*

P: I would be very grateful.

R: *Because of how painful it is?*

P: It's something that's in the past, and I don't think of it anymore that much.

R: *Have you talked to your children about it?*

P: No, no. Of course not. What's the point?

R: *Here is one point: a man had the most awful tragedy in his life when his wife and unborn child were brutally murdered. And you survive, and over the next four or five years come to grips with what happened. Then you make what many consider to be an American classic,* Chinatown. *And you think about your life and about what we talked about earlier, your mother, the Holocaust, Poland. Then this. And yet you survive and keep your sanity.*

P: Maybe.

R: *It had to do something to you, though.*

P: Well, as I already said earlier, in my opinion everything does something to you. What is a human mind if not the accumulation of experiences, daily experiences—layers and layers of them? Whatever you do is a result of this. For a psychiatrist it even shows in the doodles you do when you speak on the telephone. Filmmaking is so much more complex, it requires so much more of you. You can consider movies as some kind of an X-ray of the director's mind or soul. Even if he tries to hide he can't because it's him. And you know, if it's a very banal, mundane movie, the director shows through.

R: *So if I want to understand you, I should lock myself somewhere and watch your movies?*

P: It's not that simple. If you just watch it, as Charlie Rose, you might just enjoy the movie.

R: *But if I look at it with some considered viewpoint, I would understand.*

P: Probably, or maybe you would misunderstand. Of course, I think whatever man creates is there to be understood, whether it's today's documentary or ancient scriptures or whatever. There is a man behind it, and it depends on how good an analyst you are to get the essence out of it.

R: *Why do you think* Chinatown *was such a great movie?*

P: I haven't got a clue.

R: *Come on. It's one of the classic films of the last thirty years.*

P: Yes, but it's not a question for me.

R: *What do you mean, it's not a question for you? It's the best movie you've ever made by far. Nothing else is close.*

P: This estimation is relative. Whoever looks at the movie gets his thing out of it. Although a lot of people consider it such, you can find others who prefer something else.

R: *Do you prefer something else?*
P: I don't think I've made my movie yet. I don't have one that would give me real satisfaction. I wouldn't put any one of them on my gravestone.

R: *What's keeping you from making the movie that's your best movie?*
P: It's a question of choice of the subject. I haven't found a theme that's close or worthy enough yet. One day I will find it. Maybe my next movie will be it. That's possible. Oh, I hope.

R: *Well, is this a passion for you? Are you obsessed by this?*
P: I'm obsessed by every movie I make because once I start working on it I get so involved. Filmmaking is my toy, you know? This is my minia-ture electric train, and once I'm on the set—playing with it—nothing can distract me. It's just that I have to find something that gives me the same source of enthusiasm and at the same time is meaningful enough to be presented as something worthy. It's not only the question of the way you tell it but what you're saying that's important. I can tell the story. I know that. Technique is no problem anymore for me.

R: *So what's the problem?*
P: The problem is the subject. I hope that *The Pianist* is going to be it. I don't know to what extent, but at this moment I'm completely involved with it. I think the story says things of extreme importance, particularly today after all those years when people have begun to for-get that these things really existed, where there is a recurrence of the ideology that led to this human tragedy, of the Holocaust.

R: *The Holocaust and Nazism.*
P: Of the whole war, you know? Not only the Holocaust. That's why I used the word "tragedy" rather than "Holocaust" because "Holocaust" somehow limits it. It was a tragedy, a global tragedy.

R: *Did you think that* The Ninth Gate *could be the film?*
P: No, I thought it was a film that would be fun to make. It's the kind of subject that I enjoy very much. It's my cup of tea. It's something that gave me an opportunity to show my profession at its utmost.

R: *The story is of a man searching for two books about the Devil.*

P: No, it's really a story of a character who is a book expert and who is a mercenary and is entrusted with a book that's supposed to have some kind of supernatural qualities. Being completely materialistic, he sees profit in it and doesn't believe in the qualities that others believe this book has. But as he goes through his research, things occur that make him change his mind.

R: *I'm interested in what makes you tick. I'm interested in—*

P: I know you are. But I'm not.

R: *—why you've made the choices you have. I'm interested in why you haven't made a deal to come back to the United States, where you've got lots of friends and lots of people and where clearly the Hollywood community would welcome you. Why not? That has nothing to do with instinct. That has to do with reality.*

P: Well, one major reason is that I would immediately become prey of the media and I don't think I could go through that circus. Inevitably I would have to spend some time until things are cleared, whatever way it would go. I can't even figure myself being surrounded by prurient journalists.

R: *I'm not being prurient. I hope you'll grant me that.*

P: No, I'm not talking about you. I'm really proud of being interviewed by a man like you. I'm not giving this kind of interviews to other journalists, but you are surrounded by colleagues who are interested in other aspects of my life. They would immediately jump upon the opportunity if there's any kind of word about my returning and write some kind of article for the tabloids.

R: *But what are you scared of? What can they write or say about you that scares you?*

P: It doesn't scare me. It's just very unpleasant.

R: *All right. But unpleasant is a fact of life. I mean, maybe that's a price you have to pay.*

P: But don't you try to avoid unpleasantness?

R: *Of course you do, but at some cost. Lots of people, including your friends, believe you would only be able to achieve your potential as a filmmaker—your profession and craft of choice—if you had been able to come back. And that's in your hands, not somebody else's.*

P: But I don't know. I didn't say I'm not going to do it. Believe me, there are other much more important aspects of my possible return than you think. The most important for me would be to get it over with. It's rather for my peace of mind than any other reason.

R: *I look across at you, at someone who is all that you are: talented, you know, a survivor, tough, loving. And at the same time this thing happened that caused you to flee the country, and the young woman involved has said it was not what the press said it was.*

P: That's not important. What's important is that she says she would like me to return and get it over with.

R: *She would like you to come and get it over with. But you are not doing it, and I don't believe you will unless you can tell me this is something you want to do, and that you're willing to pay the price. And the fact that you're going to have to walk through a media maelstrom doesn't seem to me to be too high a mountain to climb. Tell me what you think.*

P: I don't know. You started by interviewing me and asking me about my childhood and my youth. I escaped from the ghetto. I lived that way. Maybe, as you said, it shaped my personality. Maybe that's what I'm subconsciously looking for: exile. You know, I remember that one of the films that really impressed me when I was a child—and I still consider it as one of the best movies I've ever seen and a film which made me want to pursue this career more than anything else— was *Odd Man Out*. I loved that movie. First of all, I loved the look of it, the construction, the atmosphere, the acting. I always dreamt of doing things of this sort or that style. To a certain extent I must say that I somehow perpetuate the ideas of that movie in what I do. You know, not long ago the film was on television and I started watching it. It was in the middle of the night. It's still fabulous, probably James Mason's best picture. And then suddenly one thing struck me that never came across my mind before. It's about the fugitive, you see? And I think that's why that film had such an impact on me when

I was a child. There's something in me. I always lived out of my country, out of the place where I should be. I always had something there which was threatening me. I always had some kind of nightmare, you know?

R: *You're not saying to me that somehow you're comfortable with this role of the fugitive and you like it?*
P: Whether I like it or not, I don't know. I'm not a masochist.

R: *No, you're more of a hedonist.*
P: I can only tell you that I live here. I'm respected here. I'm happy here. I have family. I have children. Protecting my children at this stage of my life is the most important thing. I don't want to subject them to the curiosity of the press. I don't want to be all over the tabloids. I can tell you that here in France we have very strict laws regarding privacy and even the paparazzi respect it. When I'm somewhere with my children, like for example at the Academie de Beaux Arts, I say, "Please, don't photograph my daughter," and they don't.

R: *The Academie de Beaux Art is one of the highest honors that can be given to a Frenchman or Frenchwoman. It's a select group of people. You were inducted in 1999.*
P: The induction was recently but I was elected about a year-and-a-half ago. It takes time to organize the induction because it's a big event.

R: *You seem to be saying two things. "All my life, perhaps I've been a fugitive on the outside looking in," and "I have this rather comfortable existence here."*
P: Not "rather," a very comfortable existence.

R: *"I am honored in my place of residence, Paris, France. And for those of you who think that I should go through the fire—whatever it might be— in order to return to the United States don't understand the toll it will take on my own psyche, but more importantly on my new family, which came late in life for me. And whatever is at the other side of the river is not worth crossing."*
P: It's more or less this.

R: *Tell me what you tell your children when they grow up and say, "Daddy, what happened in America?"*

P: Whatever I tell my children is always the truth. I have never lied to my children and I never will, not even about Santa Claus. About a two years ago my daughter came to me and asked me straight in the face, "Daddy, does Santa Claus exist? Or is it the parents that buy the presents?" And I said, "Look, you're asking me like that. I can't lie to you. Of course, it's parents. Santa Claus doesn't exist. It's a pity that you're asking me this question because it is such a beautiful fantasy." "Oh, don't worry about it," she says. She was about five or something, four and a half. And then she said, "Well, if it's not Santa Claus, but the parents who buy the presents, why were my rabbit boots and formal frogs two sizes too small?"

R: *Yes. Santa Claus can make that mistake, but my parents shouldn't, right?*

P: That's right.

R: *Let me just stay with this. When your daughter's thirteen years old, if she comes to you and she's read this story somewhere, what will you say when she asks, "Daddy, did you rape a thirteen-year-old? Did you have sex with a thirteen-year-old? Did you do that with someone?"*

P: Well, I'm not going to dwell on it, Charlie. I tell you, I will tell them the truth. And the truth is not what you're saying. Are you implying that I would have to explain to my children about what the press or media say? And truly, I did my time in prison. That was supposed to be it. And because the judge then reneged on the bargain-plea that was accepted by all sides and wanted me to go back, I left. And that's it. I won't go any further.

R: *I believe what you say. Your wife says about you, "The reason I love him so much in part is because I know he will always be there for me. I know he will never lie to me. I know he will always protect me." That could almost be what your children would say, too.*

P: It's a nice thing. I'm glad she says things like that about me.

R: *I hate to see that the fear of the media-trial fire prevents someone from closing the circle.*

P: But don't you realize that the media maybe took over the judicial system in your country? In any case it was all because of the media. The judge himself said at one point, "They will have what they want." You know?

R: *Your head?*

P: Yes, they wanted my head. Look, it all started so long ago. It started after *Rosemary's Baby*, after the Manson murders. There was a long period before they found the culprit where they were clearly blaming the victims for their own deaths and me for somehow being involved. The absurdity of it was so awesome, that they could suggest it had something to do with black magic or that there was a Ouija board found on the property. I remember my astonishment. I was all right with the press before that. My real problems started with the murder of Sharon Tate and they wouldn't let it go. It's all somehow mixed up with the supernatural, with the Devil. "Why do you make so many films about the Devil?" I made two: *Rosemary's Baby* and *The Ninth Gate*. My answer usually is, "Which one are you talking about? *Tess* or *Knife in the Water* or *Chinatown* or *Death and the Maiden?*"

R: *It goes back to what we said, "It's hard to make a good movie."*

P: It's very hard to make a movie, period. To make a good movie, it's really a question of luck, I would say.

R: *Why is it so difficult to make a good movie?*

P: It's a tremendously complex form of art. It just doesn't depend only on your canvas and paint and paints and colors and brushes. You need an army around you, you need means of production and all the hardware. What's difficult about it? I'll tell you. It's made of pieces, and to maintain the coherence between those pieces is difficult. When a director intends to make a movie, he's got the model of it in his head and the making the movie consists of making that model available to others. There are a lot of people who imagine beautifully, except nobody else knows they're imagining. Directing is making this imagination physical, material. After all, at the end of the day it's only a piece of film on a reel. When you start doing it there are so many elements you are using that you get further and further away from the model you have in your head.

First there is the choice of the actors. You imagined certain characters, you're trying to be as close as possible, but there are other options that you come across which are not necessarily like the ones you had. An actor is very popular at the moment, for example, and the studio wants him. But he's not what you thought. Sometimes when you're lucky enough you can be as close in reality to what you imagined. There is a physical reality in which the scene will happen, like a room. And that room, even if you build it in the studio, even according to your instructions and plans, is not exactly like the one you imagined. I personally try to concentrate and remember that first vision, that first conception which I liked so much, and see how it relates to this new reality that superimposes itself on my imagined movie. The closer I am to it, the better off I am in the end. And sometimes I literally stand on the set, close my eyes, and try to remember how I imagined the scene before the casting, before the arguing with the producers, before the talk about money, before hiring the actors.

When you're doing the film, you don't—as everyone knows—do it in continuity. You do it in pieces, and there are so many elements to distract you that, when you put it all together, it's not what it's supposed to be. Rushes always look great—even in mediocre films, everybody's always happy. The tragic moment is the rough cut when you put it all together for the first time. Usually the director goes to rest for a few weeks and leaves it with the editor to put it all together. Sometimes he goes to a clinic. Then he returns and sits, and the projection starts. This is the moment when he wants to hang himself because almost inevitably it looks terrible, even with all my experience— and I've been doing this for years and years. So that's why it's so difficult. It's difficult because it's a mosaic of things, because you don't see the whole thing. I went to art school and I know you're supposed to draft the whole thing and then go to the details. Filmmaking is the opposite. You start with the details and then you put it all together.

R: *It's almost incomprehensible that you can do that because it seems to me that you go from the forest to the trees, rather than from the trees to the forest.*

P: That's exactly what it is.

R: *If Polanski is about two things: love and work. Yes? Your life and your passions. What do your regret? What would you change? What would you have done differently about your life?*

P: What would I have done differently about my life? I don't know. Maybe I should have been acting more.

R: *Oh, come on. That's not what you believe. That's silly. You were born to direct.*

P: Yes, but that question, I think, deserves the answer I gave you because how can you ask me what would I have done differently? As Democritus said, "Everything in the universe is the fruit of chance and necessity." And life, it's something between what you need and what is available. You see? In other words, "You can't always get what you want," as the Rolling Stones sing. You're going somewhere. You desire certain things. And, of course, you make mistakes on the way. I can't regret my mistakes. It would be silly. Though I do acknowledge them.

R: *It's great to see you in Paris. Thank you very much.*

P: Thank you. It was a very interesting, stimulating moment. And I wish it could go on.

R: *Perhaps in the United States.*

P: Perhaps, perhaps.

Memories of the Ghetto

OCTAVI MARTI/2001

THE FILM DIRECTOR ROMAN POLANSKI and the writer
Jorge Semprun greet and hug each other warmly, then begin an absorb-
ing but sensitive conversation. They are talking about Polanski's new
film, *The Pianist*, which is set in the Warsaw ghetto and which won the
Palme D'Or at the Cannes Film Festival. Both men lived through the
horrors of Nazi genocide.

Roman Polanski made his position clear from the outset: "I'm not
interested in giving interviews. I don't want to analyze anything,
including myself." He was only prepared to talk to "a colleague and
someone from the same generation as mine." That person didn't necessarily have to be a filmmaker, only someone who knows what it means
to have escaped the Shoah, someone who suffered at the hands of the
Nazis and who understands the difference between the ghetto, the concentration camp, and the extermination camp. Jorge Semprun was the
man for the job. A survivor of Buchenwald himself, he is also an accomplished writer and occasional filmmaker.

Meeting in the Paris office of the French-Polish director on an
extremely noisy autumn morning, they avoided the more sensitive topics
from the start as a carpenter drilled away on the floor underneath them.

P: I look on the screenplay as an instruction manual on how to tell the
story. I can't imagine being on location without having collaborated on
writing those instructions. Sometimes I've adapted a story or a set of

From *El País Semanal*, 1 December 2001. © Diario El País. S. L. Reprinted by permission.
Translated by Remi Guillochon and Paul Cronin.

events myself. On other occasions I've co-written the script, and in the best instances have participated in the development of the script without any credit. This was the case with *The Pianist* which I worked on with Ronald Harwood under ideal conditions. We were staying at a house near Paris, enjoying fine weather and taking long walks. The children played in the garden, we had a fabulous cook at work in the kitchen, and my wife came home every night from the theater where she was performing. We'd get up very early and discuss what Harwood had written the day before and I'd suggest possible changes. Then we'd go for a walk, review the story and go through the next sequences. Harwood would take a little nap after lunch so his mind would be fresh for working in front of the computer. It still mystifies me when I receive a script written by someone I don't know. I'm expected to make a film of it without knowing anything about where it comes from.

s: *With* The Pianist *you had to relive a very harrowing period of your life, something that required complete personal involvement.*
p: That's right. The difficulty was not working for ten to twelve hours a day on the project, but having to work on such a personal story, one that was bottled up inside. I always said I wanted to make a film about that particular period of my life—or at least the immediate postwar era—but I didn't want it to be autobiographical. Harwood and I used documentary footage that was sent to us from Warsaw, as well as Wladyslaw Szpilman's book, for source material. The footage contained images of the destroyed city, the ghetto, and all those horrible events. It was hard to see things like that again and relive those years. We got through it by working with a positive attitude, laughing a lot, making bad jokes, and talking about the hundreds of Jews we had to kill off in the next scene. We didn't adopt this way of doing things deliberately— it was more instinctive than that.

s: *Humor is one way of coping with these horrors. I admire* The Pianist's *intellectual honesty, the way it doesn't use any gimmicks or tricks.*
p: From the beginning I knew I had to tell the story in the first person and that I couldn't compromise on this. We had to overcome the inevitable problems this approach entailed. I'd thought about re-creating

the events in black and white for the film but realized this would be even more unnatural than using color. The film wasn't going to be a star vehicle so I needed unknown faces. I began by holding a series of casting sessions in London but then came across some tapes of Adrien Brody and gave him the role. I also promised myself from day one that I wouldn't use close-ups in the opening shots, which meant I couldn't win over the audience through sentimental and gimmicky tricks. The camera had to be invisible. And I didn't want to include documentary style filmmaking with the sort of shaky and unclear images you'd get if the Pope himself were filming. This all required considerable intellectual honesty. When I sat around this very table with my co-producers Alain Sarde and Robert Benmussa, we immediately agreed on one important principle: how we would work together on *The Pianist*. With absolute integrity and sincerity all the way, something that came through in different ways. In Germany and Poland the entire technical team and all the extras were happy to work fourteen hours a day. They knew they were contributing to something out of the ordinary that wasn't going to make a fortune. The combination of subject and filmmaker attracted the right kind of people.

s: *It was your job to tell Spzilman's story as well as you possibly could.*
P: What makes Szpilman's book stand out is its detached style. Everything is contained in the book, and the film remains very faithful to his language despite the change of form. Once we'd finished the film there was nothing more to add. That's why I haven't given many interviews about it. Poets never analyze and deconstruct their work—they don't explain the meaning of every single word.

Polanski came across the Szpilman book quite by chance, thanks to a friend. Szpilman, who wrote his book in 1945 while he was still living his own private wartime nightmare, was a professional pianist working on Warsaw Radio when the Nazis invaded Poland in 1939. Together with his parents, two sisters, and brother he moved to the newly established ghetto, an area of the city where 360,000 Jews had been crammed together, a figure that rose to half a million when the deported Jews from neighboring countries moved in. 100,000 of them died of hunger or typhus and more than 300,000 were sent to the death camps. Between April and May 1943, with no more than 200 weapons among them, 40,000 took part in the Warsaw uprising, which lasted for a month. By January 1945, when the Germans abandoned the city to the Soviet Army, only twenty Jews were still alive in Warsaw. One of them was Szpilman who had survived through the help of a few friends and the unexpected intervention of a German officer named Wim Hosenfeld. A Catholic serviceman who saved a large number of Poles—both Jewish and non-Jewish—this didn't stop Hosenfeld from being tortured by the Soviets and dying in the Gulag. Though Szpilman's book was published in 1946, the authorities removed it from circulation because his account didn't describe every Pole, Lithuanian, Ukrainian, and Jew as heroic. Some were sadistic and many were traitors or cowards who decided to ignore what they saw around them, which to the Stalinist regime was an unacceptable portrayal.

P: Today's generation usually thinks of the ghetto as a concentration camp, when actually it was a closed-off area encircled by walls with streets and houses, cafés and restaurants, rich and poor people who were both calm and hysterical. There were even schools and workshops in Theresienstadt. Some people were clearly better off than others. The recorded images of the ghetto are, of course, unbearable to look at. There are dead bodies in the streets and people dying from disease and hunger. But there are also people who appear well fed. The footage shot by the Germans was intended to show the world that there wasn't much solidarity among the Jews. The ghetto came before the concentration camps. Before it was liquidated things were deteriorating bit by bit, even though people still thought their situation might improve. I wanted to show this gradual breakdown in the film. First a new law was passed that limited the amount of money that Jews could keep. Then they were banned from using public benches, and then they had to walk on the edge of the pavement and were forced to wear the Star of David. Thinking about it now, at a safe distance, it's easy to ask why didn't they stand up and fight. But it's foolish of people to think that real life works like it does in films. Organizing a rebellion is no easy matter. It was a hell on earth in the ghetto.

s: *How did you come across Szpilman's book? It has given you the opportu-*
nity to refer, indirectly, to your childhood, to put everything you know into
the story without having to talk about yourself in the first person.
p: The book was reedited in Germany by Szpilman's son in 1998
before it was published in English, and a lawyer friend of mine in
London gave me a copy. I started to read it but it's actually not that well
written and, at first, I thought it was just one more book about the Nazi
occupation. Some time later Gene Gutowski, who produced *Cul-de-sac*
and *The Fearless Vampire Killers*, gave me a call and persuaded me to
take another look at it.

The Pianist let me make use of what I went through in Krakow without having to interpret it or be autobiographical. I know what Szpilman
is talking about—he brings my past back to me. Though the subject
matter is bleak, it's treated objectively and with real detachment, which
is what I like about the book. It's also a very positive story in the way
that the person telling it is himself a survivor. Szpilman's book makes a
very strong impression through the details, something that's characteristic of his direct writing style. It has that peculiar brand of precision
and distance that the survivor often carries with him.

s: *I watched your film as if I were hearing the testimony of someone who*
escaped the extermination camps. The narrative is in the first person, which
makes audiences feel as if they are right inside the story.
p: When I was standing on set with Gene Gutowski, who also experienced life in the ghetto and the ruins of postwar Poland, both of us
suddenly felt transported back to that era. The sense of reality was
astonishing. We filmed in a derelict district on the outskirts of Warsaw
where until a few years ago there were large industrial plants from
Soviet times which are now in ruins. The difference is that when you
see documentary images from that period, you know the people behind
the cameras were Nazis and you can't help feeling uneasy about it all.
When I showed the production team archive footage they weren't terribly bothered that somebody had filmed these things. But I still can't
understand just who could be capable of documenting such indescrib-
able misery and not lose their mind.

My mother died in Auschwitz and my uncle died in Buchenwald, but
my father managed to survive Mauthausen. Just a few weeks ago I was

in Tel Aviv looking at the extensive archives they have there. Someone had told me about some filing cabinets that had been discovered a few years before in London which contain typed record-cards of the prisoners from Mauthausen. I went down to the archives to look for my father's card. Everything was organized by nationality, and as I walked around these boxes full of papers it was as though I were walking through the opening scenes of *Citizen Kane*. I found my father's card which was in mint condition, though it had yellowed a little bit. It gave a detailed description of his appearance, including hair and eye color, his size, but it didn't mention his weight. In the record-card he states he has no children—I had escaped the ghetto—and gives his age as six years younger than he actually was, though that still made him too old to be considered for work. He passed himself off as a locksmith.

S: *A German prisoner who wanted to protect me wrote on my card from Buchenwald that I was a plasterer instead of a student. He knew that people with few qualifications and manual jobs had more chance of getting work in the camp, and so had an increased chance of survival. If I had been classified as a student, I would have been sent to the next camp of Dora where the underground launch pads for the V1 and V2 rockets were located. The living conditions were very harsh and no one lasted for very long there.*

P: My father explained how in Mathausen he chose the stone he had to carry to the top of an outside staircase. He tried to pick a large, flat slab so that it weighed less and offered some protection against the Nazis who amused themselves by throwing stones at the prisoners. When he met up with fellow deportees after the war and they talked about their experiences—which didn't happen very often—they remembered what it felt like going up those stairs. My father made himself look ridiculous when he mimed the gestures he made in front of the guards. I couldn't stand it when he did that, it made me feel ashamed of him. But he and his friends treated this routine as something grotesque and would laugh about it.

Roman Polanski was able to meet with the children of Wim Hosenfeld, the serviceman who hid and fed Szpilman during the final stages of the

Nazi occupation of Warsaw. While the SS were putting an end to the Warsaw uprising in June 1943, Hosenfeld wrote in his diary, "Those mobsters think they can win the war like this, but they don't realize that this senseless massacre of the Jews has already lost us the war. We have filled ourselves with shame. It will always hang over us. We deserve no pity. We are all guilty."

P: Hosenfeld's five children—three daughters and two sons, who are now in their sixties—came to see the film in Berlin. We drank some champagne in the Kempinski hotel together: the surviving children of the Wehrmacht officer sitting alongside the survivor from the ghetto. They were very moved by the film. The photograph that Thomas Kretschmann—the actor who plays Hosenfeld—has on his table in the film, is a real photo of the Hosenfeld family with the actor's face superimposed over Hosenfeld's. And do you know what? In the first version of the book Hosenfeld is depicted as being Austrian rather than German because people couldn't accept that you could have a good German. Though the Austrians always claim they have been invaded in the past, they forget just how enthusiastic Vienna was about becoming part of Hitler's Germany, and even that Kurt Waldheim was able to pass himself off as having fought against the Nazis.

There Were Four of Us

LEON DE WINTER/2002

THE GREAT ACTOR WALTER MATTHAU once said to me,
"Roman, you're always telling me Jewish jokes—but they're anti-Semitic."
I said, "How can you say that, Walter? Laughing at ourselves has always
been one of the great strength of Jewish culture. Even in the ghetto we
told each other Jewish jokes." Matthau said, "Don't tell me about the
ghetto—I know what kind of jokes they told there." I asked, "How do
you know that?" "I was in the ghetto too," he said. "Excuse me, Walter,
I didn't know you'd been in the ghetto. Which one?" Matthau said,
"I grew up in the New York ghetto." Now, Matthau had a great sense
of humor, but he meant this quite seriously. I like telling Jewish jokes.
They're the funniest—it's really where our strength lies. We're probably
the only people who don't get too upset with ourselves.

At home we weren't even practicing Jews. Judaism first began to
play a role during the war when we all had to wear a white armband
with a Star of David on it. Only then did I begin to understand that I
was different from other children. But my parents were completely
assimilated and the only really Jewish thing about us was that we
celebrated Passover. My grandmother clung to the tradition and I went
with her to the synagogue a few times, but otherwise we weren't any
different from everyone around us. We didn't dress any differently, we
didn't talk differently, I didn't play differently from other children.
In Le Monde some idiot wrote that there weren't enough characters

From Die Welt, 30 November 2002. Reprinted by permission of Leon de Winter.
Translated by Joshua Kronen and Paul Cronin.

wearing traditional clothes in *The Pianist*, that there were too few yarmulkas and beards. He obviously has no idea how Jews looked in the ghetto during the war. They weren't any different from other people, apart from the fact that they got poorer and poorer. He probably thought everyone was running around looking like Hasidim.

I remember only one Hasidic family in the ghetto. They lived across from us on the other side of the street and had a son who dressed in orthodox clothing, just like the fanatics you see at the Wailing Wall. As kids we were always making fun of him, like cruel children tend to do. We would run after him and pull on his locks. One time a friend of mine wondered where we could make holy water so we could baptize the guy and make him a Christian, but I hadn't a clue how to turn normal water into holy water. The point is that the vast majority of the Jewish population in Poland was fully integrated.

We lived in Krakow but then suddenly had to move to another neighborhood in the city. It wasn't cordoned off yet—they built the walls later, something I can remember very vividly. I show it in *The Pianist*, although it isn't described in Szpilman's book. My sister called me to the window and pointed outside, saying, "Look over there." The two of us were alone—our parents weren't around—and it was at this moment I understood that things had become serious. They'd actually built a wall. I remember standing next to my sister and crying.

What I wanted to show in the film was the gradual development of the events that ultimately led to the death camps and gas chambers. It began with simple things like Jews not being allowed to sit on park benches. People often ask me, "Why didn't the Jews do something to stop what was happening?" But it's an absurd question. At the time we thought, "It can't get any worse. It can only get better."

The Germans cleared a neighborhood in Krakow that had been occupied by Christians in order to concentrate the Jews in a single area. It wasn't a traditional Jewish quarter. We moved into a large apartment which we had to share with four or five other families. At first we had two rooms and a common kitchen, but later more families moved in and we only had one room. There were four of us: my parents, my sister, and I. It was relatively easy to deal with, that is until the raids began when they started taking people away. The ghetto became smaller and smaller, and they put up barbed wire fences.

Both my parents worked outside the ghetto. My mother was a cleaner in the office of the *Generalgouvernement* in the Königspalast. I stayed at home with my sister and spent the day playing outside in the street with other children. After a while we had to move again. This time we lived with a married couple and their three- or four-year-old son, and a man and his dog called Viefka. It was pretty bad, but not unbearable. The ghetto in Krakow was never as terrible as the one in Warsaw. They cleared it before people started to die of hunger and Jews were never brought in from outside the city. The Warsaw ghetto initially had 360,000 people and at its peak housed half a million. People who had absolutely nothing and who were already severely malnourished were forced to live there. They just died in the streets and the cellars.

I don't know if you've seen any of the films shot in the ghetto, but they're really quite unimaginable. People wearing rags are barely aware that the Germans are pointing a camera at them. The footage is so moving that you forget there must have been someone on the other side of the camera.

A few times I managed to sneak out of the ghetto. As a child it was easy to slip through the barbed wire. One time my mother took me to some people whom I was supposed to stay with but whom I'd never met before. I don't know how she managed to sort this out, but I guessed she had permission to be outside the ghetto because she worked in the Königspalast. My father had given them money and some of our things. My father picked me up and took me back to the ghetto. On the way home he told me that my mother had been taken in a raid. We were walking over a bridge and he began to cry, and I told him that he shouldn't cry because he wasn't wearing a Jewish star around his arm, which was illegal. I was scared they would catch us. The Germans had lists—they didn't take away people arbitrarily. The idea was to break up families, and one day they came for my sister. I don't know why they wanted her, perhaps because she was young and could work or something like that. One time they came to our house but my mother had hidden her.

We had to move again. The Germans had reduced the size of the ghetto even more and they had taken away the parents of a little boy called Stephan who lived in the same house, so my father and I looked after him.

One time we found a room in a courtyard. We had the feeling that the final liquidation of the ghetto was about to take place, but it didn't actually happen at that point. Then I left the ghetto once more, though I don't know for how long. I went back to the family outside where I'd been before. When I got back in the ghetto, a raid had just taken place. It was a warm, sunny day. The ghetto was surrounded, I think by Ukrainians. Men in black uniforms—they were the worst of the lot. I managed to get to the small room in the courtyard. It was little more than a shack where we lived.

This part of the ghetto was completely abandoned. The scene in *The Pianist* where the main character walks completely alone through an abandoned street with various objects strewn about—furniture and clothes and such—is what it really looked like. There wasn't anyone around. The entire neighborhood was empty and had been turned completely upside down. But all I wanted to do was find my father.

From a distance I saw them taking people from a building. There were one or two Jewish ghetto guards and a German with a list of names in his hand. A small group of people were standing there ready to be taken away. There were no more than fifteen in total. I went over to them and someone asked me if I was crazy. "I'm following everyone else," I said. They made us march to the Umschlagplatz in Krakow, a large square where hundreds or maybe thousands of people were waiting. I looked desperately for my father but didn't see him anywhere. I did find little Stephan though. I quickly realized I'd made a mistake by going there and started to think about how I could get away. The only possibility was to speak to one of the Polish guards standing among the crowd. I went over to one of the younger ones and, holding Stephan's hand, I told him we were terribly hungry and that we wanted to run home and get some bread. From the way he looked at us it was clear he knew we wanted to escape. He said, "Alright, go." I grabbed Stephan and began to run. "Don't run," he shouted. That line is in the film.

We snuck from one courtyard to another—they were all connected and I knew them like the back of my hand. We went to the family outside of the ghetto who said, "Now we've got *two* small Jews." We stayed, I think, only a single night there. I just wanted to see my father. The most terrible thing that can happen to a child is to be separated from his parents. Later on, I suffered more from missing my parents than from hunger.

I returned to the ghetto with Stephan and found my father. I don't know exactly how much time passed before the ghetto was liquidated. Specific events, yes, but the chronology is a problem. Stephan and I had to work in the ghetto which had gotten smaller. We glued paper bags. I can still show you how it's done. When we filmed *The Pianist* I showed the prop man how to do it. You take a piece of paper and fold it this way, then this way, then you glue it on this side together, and you've got a bag. I was a little older but poor Stephan also had to make these damn paper bags. You know, before I had kids myself I could see things from a child's perspective. As a child you don't complain—children are quite resilient. But today I consider things from a father's point of view and find it much harder to think about these times, when before I would see Stephan in my mind and laugh.

Finally the end of the ghetto came. At five in the morning my father took me out to the barbed wire fence. I hadn't told him that I'd actually snuck in and out before, since it had been very dangerous. Once I'd even slipped out to buy stamps in a store for my stamp collection. My father cut the hole in the barbed wire not far from the main entrance and said, "Go." And so I went, all alone. Stephan stayed in the ghetto. They shot him in the schoolyard with other children. Back then they killed all the children. I went back to the family but no one was home, so I decided to go back to the ghetto.

When I was close I saw the Germans with a column of men marching through the street. My father was among them. I ran beside them, along the sidewalk, where my father noticed me. He was walking near a guard and very cleverly slipped back two rows in the column to distance himself from the guard. I remember how much it impressed me that he could communicate with the other men in the column without uttering a word. I was able to make it clear to him that the family wasn't at home and the door was locked. "Go away!" he whispered.

That was the last time I saw my father during the war. He survived, but my stamp collection—which I'd risked my life for—is lost. It wasn't worth much anyhow. I was still a child.

INDEX

CONVERSATIONS WITH FILMMAKERS SERIES

PETER BRUNETTE, GENERAL EDITOR

The collected interviews with notable modern directors, including

Robert Aldrich • Pedro Almodóvar • Robert Altman • Theo Angelopolous • Bernardo Bertolucci • Tim Burton • Jane Campion • Frank Capra • Charlie Chaplin • Francis Ford Coppola • George Cukor • Brian De Palma • Clint Eastwood • John Ford • Terry Gilliam • Jean-Luc Godard • Peter Greenaway • Alfred Hitchcock • John Huston • Jim Jarmusch • Elia Kazan • Stanley Kubrick • Fritz Lang • Spike Lee • Mike Leigh • George Lucas • Sidney Lumet • Michael Powell • Jean Renoir • Martin Ritt • Carlos Saura • John Sayles • Martin Scorsese • Ridley Scott • Steven Soderbergh • Steven Spielberg • George Stevens • Oliver Stone • Quentin Tarantino • Lars von Trier • Orson Welles • Billy Wilder • John Woo • Zhang Yimou • Fred Zinnemann